The One-Minute
Apologist

Also by Dave Armstrong
from Sophia Institute Press®:

A Biblical Defense of Catholicism
The Catholic Verses

Dave Armstrong

The One-Minute Apologist

Essential Catholic Replies
to Over Sixty Common Protestant Claims

SOPHIA INSTITUTE PRESS®
Manchester, New Hampshire

Biblical citations are taken from the Revised Standard Version of the Bible (© 1971 by Division of Christian Education of the National Council of the Churches of Christ in the United States of America), unless otherwise noted. All emphases added.

All citations from the Church Fathers are taken from the 38-volume set of patristic writings (in the public domain), edited by Philip Schaff (1887).

For further related reading, see the author's award-winning website: Biblical Evidence for Catholicism (http://www.biblicalcatholic.com), and particularly the web pages:

Protestantism:

http://ic.net/~erasmus/RAZ387.HTM

Martin Luther and Lutheranism:

http://ic.net/~erasmus/LUTHERANISM.HTM

John Calvin and Calvinism:

http://ic.net/~erasmus/CALVINISM.HTM

Sacred Scripture and Sacred Tradition

http://ic.net/~erasmus/ERASMUS3.HTM

The Church

http://ic.net/~erasmus/RAZ12.HTM

Sophia Institute Press®

Box 5284, Manchester, NH 03108

1-800-888-9344

www.sophiainstitute.com

Library of Congress Cataloging-in-Publication Data

Armstrong, Dave, 1958-

The one-minute apologist : essential Catholic replies to over sixty Protestant claims / by Dave Armstrong.

   p. cm.

Includes bibliographical references.

ISBN-13: 978-1-933184-23-4 (pbk. : alk. paper)

ISBN-10: 1-933184-23-X (pbk. : alk. paper) 1. Catholic Church — Apologetic works. 2. Catholic Church — Relations — Protestant churches. 3. Protestant churches — Relations — Catholic Church. I. Title.

BX1752.A77 2007

230′.2 — dc22   2006103357

10 11 12 11 10 9 8 7 6 5 4

To my friends, esteemed fellow apologists,
and all those who seek to "give
answer for the hope that is in them"
and to help others to better understand
the one, holy, catholic, and apostolic Church

"I have become all things to all men, that I might by all means save some."

1 Corinthians 9:22

Contents

The Papacy

The Priesthood

The Sacraments

Other Topics

✠

Introduction

This book continues what might be called a "Bible and Catholicism" trilogy (the previous two volumes being *A Biblical Defense of Catholicism* and *The Catholic Verses*).

The first was geared more toward a "catechetical" approach: a positive presentation of the basic teachings of Catholics that are different from most Protestant denominations, along with the biblical rationale for them (our proof texts, so to speak).

The second dealt with a similar theme, but with a twist: focusing on the ways in which Protestants have traditionally tried to deal with Bible texts that support Catholic teachings, and how these (oftentimes quite desperate) counter-explanations fail to meet the mark. This book was more "polemical" in its approach, featuring arguments against Catholicism, and our replies.

In this work, I have sought to show how Catholics can easily, decisively answer non-Catholic "garden-variety" objections to Catholicism. To do so, I have adopted a standard format (very vaguely reminiscent of St. Thomas Aquinas's *Summa Theologica*) throughout the entire book:

1. The topic title is stated in one or two lines. Remember — this is the Protestant *objection* to Catholic teaching, not my own assertion!

2. I provide the essential Catholic replies to the objection.

3. A common follow-up argument — "A Protestant Might Further Object" — and my counter-reply.

4. A relevant citation, often from a Protestant source.

This is all done in no more than two pages for each topic.

Once again I have happily been made quite aware of both the extraordinary riches of Holy Scripture itself (I discovered many "new" and exciting passages that gave further support to Catholic views) and how compellingly its teachings harmonize with the Catholic Faith. This is one of the somewhat unique blessings of the Catholic apologist. During the course of defending the Church and her teachings, the apologist sees more and more that our explanations make perfect sense and that opposing ones are weighed down and made implausible or incoherent by serious deficiencies (both biblical and logical).

As a former Protestant, I am particularly delighted by this (as I suspect is the case with other converts and also lifelong Catholics who have had a lot of contact with Protestants or familiarity with Protestant distinctives). For many years, I had assumed that Protestantism was "obviously" more biblically grounded than Catholicism.

My goal has been to provide readers with a handy, concise reference work to be used in the proverbial "encounter with an evangelist at the door" or at the workplace, or with non-Catholic relatives, and so forth. If and when a non-Catholic inquires about or strongly opposes some Catholic teaching, this "pocket book" might be of some practical use.

It should be noted here that my use of the word "Protestant" is very broad. In most cases, I have in mind traditional, conservative, or evangelical Protestants, but in a few instances, the term applies (in context) to more "progressive" strains of the spectrum, encompassing an array of belief that includes theologically liberal denominations and even quasi-Christian sects like the Mormons, Jehovah's Witnesses, and Unitarians.

A final personal note: I've been known, in some Internet circles, for writing lengthy tomes on my website and blog. I don't regret doing that at all, but I must say that I now more fully appreciate the importance and utility of short treatments as well, in order to provide effective Catholic replies to those arguments against our Faith that we encounter most frequently. I hope and pray that the present effort will be helpful in that way, and that my answers provide a lot of "meat" and substance within the brief format.

The One-Minute Apologist

Scripture

The Bible is the only infallible source of theological truth

The Bible itself says so, and didn't Jesus condemn the traditions of men?

THE ONE-MINUTE APOLOGIST SAYS:
The Bible actually teaches that authoritative Christian teaching comes through the Bible, the Church,[1] *and the apostolic "deposit" or Tradition.*

Oftentimes, within a sort of Protestant "tradition," it is uncritically accepted that certain passages prove something, when in fact, a closer examination shows otherwise. This belief in "Bible Alone," or *Sola Scriptura*, is a classic example.

Scripture certainly is a "standard of truth," even the preeminent one, but not in a sense that rules out the binding authority of apostolic Tradition and the Church. Catholics agree that every true doctrine can be found in the Bible, if only indirectly sometimes, and cannot contradict it. 2 Timothy 3:16-17 ("All scripture is inspired by God and profitable for teaching, for reproof, for correction, and for training in righteousness, that the man of God may be complete, equipped for every good work") does not teach "Bible Alone," but simply describes the virtues of Holy Scripture.

Biblical indications for the Catholic position are quite numerous. When Jesus condemns "tradition,"[2] He usually qualifies His rebuke by referring to corruptions or "traditions of men." The apostle Paul refers positively to a Christian Tradition ("maintain the traditions even as I have delivered them to you"),[3] contrasting it, as Jesus did, with bad tradition ("according to human tradition . . . not according to Christ").[4] He also upholds the authority of oral Tradition, referring to "the word of God which you heard from us"[5] and "sound words which you have heard from me."[6] The latter passage is very important because it is located in the context of the 2 Timothy passage that is the most common Protestant proof text against tradition. Clearly, then, one must interpret Paul by understanding his teaching in its totality.

Perhaps the clearest biblical proof of the infallible authority of the Church is the Jerusalem Council,[7] and its authoritative, binding pronouncement:

> **Acts 15:29-30:** "For it has seemed good to the Holy Spirit and to us to lay upon you no greater burden than these necessary things: that you abstain from what has been sacrificed to idols and from blood and from what is strangled and from unchastity."

In the next chapter, we learn that Paul, Timothy, and Silas traveled around "through the cities" and "delivered to them for observance the decisions which had been reached by the apostles and elders who were at Jerusalem."[8] This is binding Church authority — with the sanction of the Holy Spirit Himself — and an explicit proof of the gift of infallibility that the Catholic Church claims for itself when assembled in a council.

A PROTESTANT MIGHT FURTHER OBJECT:

The Catholic still cannot explain why it is that Jesus and the apostles always referred to Holy Scripture to prove their doctrine. They didn't appeal to Tradition, and the Old Testament Jews also held to Bible Alone *(Sola Scriptura)*. The entire Bible bears witness to this rule of faith.

THE ONE-MINUTE APOLOGIST SAYS:

In Matthew 23:2-3, Jesus teaches that the scribes and Pharisees have a legitimate, binding authority (even when they are being rank hypocrites): "The scribes and the Pharisees sit on Moses' seat; so practice and observe whatever they tell you." The idea of "Moses' Seat" cannot be found anywhere in the Old Testament, but it appears in the (originally oral) *Mishna,* which teaches a sort of "teaching succession" from Moses on down. Also, in Matthew 2:23: the reference to "He shall be called a Nazarene" is absent from the Old Testament, yet it had been passed down (orally) "by the prophets." In 1 Corinthians 10:4, St. Paul refers to a rock that "followed" the Jews through the Sinai wilderness. In the related passages about Moses striking the rock to produce water,[9] the Old Testament doesn't say anything about such miraculous movement. But rabbinic tradition does.

Nor did the Jews ever accept *Sola Scriptura.* Only the skeptical Sadducees rejected oral Tradition, but they also rejected the future resurrection, the soul, the afterlife, eternal rewards and retribution, and demons and angels. The nature of authority in Old Testament times is illustrated by Ezra, a priest and scribe who taught the Jewish Law to Israel. His authority was binding, under pain of imprisonment, banishment, loss of goods, and even death.[10]

Therefore, the overwhelming weight of relevant biblical data is opposed to the central Protestant doctrine of Bible Alone, or *Sola Scriptura*, and strongly supports the idea of authoritative tradition.

✠

"This testimony of the universal holy Christian Church, even if we had nothing else, would be a sufficient warrant for holding this article [on the sacrament] and refusing to suffer or listen to a sectary, for it is dangerous and fearful to hear or believe anything against the unanimous testimony, belief, and teaching of the universal holy Christian churches, unanimously held in all the world from the beginning until now over fifteen hundred years."

MARTIN LUTHER

---

[1] 1 Tim 3:15 [2] e.g., Mk. 7:8-13 [3] 1 Cor. 11:2 [4] Col. 2:8 [5] 1 Thess. 2:13 [6] 2 Tim 1:13-14 [7] Acts 15:6-30 [8] Acts 16:14 [9] Ex. 17:1-7; Num. 20:2-13 [10] Ezra 7:6, 10, 25-26

The Bible is clear, or "perspicuous," in all its broad teachings about salvation

The individual with his Bible has all that's necessary to be saved. He doesn't need a church or "tradition."

THE ONE-MINUTE APOLOGIST SAYS:
The Bible does not teach this doctrine. And the history of Protestantism, with its many doctrinal divisions, argues strongly against it. How could a perspicuous Bible lead so many believers to so many different interpretations?

The Bible is not always easy to understand. It's a complex book whose words and ideas have captivated the world's most brilliant minds for millennia. Without an authoritative voice of interpretation — like a Church — error and division are inevitable.

Such division appeared right at the beginning of Protestantism. Martin Luther believed in a Real Presence of Christ in the Eucharist, but John Calvin accepted a "mystical presence" only, while Huldreich Zwingli thought it was completely symbolic. They all read the same Bible, and professed the same belief in *sola Scriptura,* but the Bible alone was not sufficient to reconcile the matter.

Baptism is another example. Luther (again closest to Catholic doctrine) believed in baptismal regeneration; Calvin and Zwingli rejected it, but agreed with Luther that infants should be baptized. The Anabaptist movement, however, thought that only adult believers should be baptized (and Lutherans and Calvinists persecuted them for it). Later on, other Protestant groups did not baptize at all (Quakers, Salvation Army) or believed in regenerative adult baptism (Church of Christ), so that there are today five major competing doctrines of baptism. Protestants also differ among themselves in many other major areas of doctrine and practice, despite their belief in one and the same "perspicuous" Bible: limited atonement versus universal atonement; whether it's possible to lose salvation; church government and female clergy; the relation of sanctification to justification; the role of the charismatic gifts, and others.

One of the strongest scriptural indications against the doctrine of biblical perspicuity can be found in 2 Peter 3:15-17:

> So also our beloved brother Paul wrote to you according to the wisdom given him, speaking of this as he does in all his letters. There are some things in them hard to understand, which the ignorant and unstable twist to their own destruction, as they do the other scriptures. You therefore,

beloved, knowing this beforehand, beware lest you be carried away with the error of lawless men and lose your own stability.[1]

A Protestant Might Further Object:

It's still better to have the freedom to believe what we find in the Bible, than to be told what to believe. Furthermore, Christians of different denominations may freely disagree about unessential doctrines, but on the essential matters of faith they usually agree. When they do disagree, though, it is because of their human sin and pride, not because the Bible's meaning isn't clear.

The One-Minute Apologist Says:

Both baptism (according to 1 Peter 3:21) and the Eucharist (John 6:53) are certainly "essential" — indeed, necessary — for salvation.

And even in seeming "non-essentials," God wills that we be unified in faith. Our Lord Jesus prayed in John 17:22, "that they may be one even as we are one." Acts 4:32 informs us that the earliest Christians were "of one heart and soul." St. Paul taught that "there is one body and one Spirit . . . one Lord, one faith, one baptism,"[2] and that Christians were to "stand firm in one spirit, with one mind striving side by side for the faith of the gospel,"[3] and to be "in full accord and of one mind."[4] St. Peter urges us to have "unity of spirit."[5] Denominationalism and doctrinal relativism are roundly condemned by the Apostle Paul:

> **1 Corinthians 1:10-13:** "I appeal to you, brethren, by the name of our Lord Jesus Christ, that all of you agree and that there be no dissensions among you, but that you be united in the same mind and the same judgment. For it has been reported to me by Chloe's people that there is quarreling among you, my brethren. What I mean is that each one of you says, 'I belong to Paul,' or 'I belong to Apollos,' or 'I belong to Cephas,' or 'I belong to Christ.' Is Christ divided? Was Paul crucified for you? Or were you baptized in the name of Paul?"

Only an authoritative Church, commissioned by Christ to teach His truth and protected by the Holy Spirit from doctrinal error, can preserve individual Christians from the dissensions caused by their own flawed interpretations, and ensure the unity for which both Christ and St. Paul prayed.

☩

"No one is trying to be dishonest. Everyone claims to be hearing the Word of God. But the indisputable fact of the matter is that Lutherans, Presbyterians, sectarians, liberals, conservatives, East Lansingites, East Berliners, southern Americans, southern Afrikaners, Indonesians, and Ghanians, all read the same Scriptures and all hear different things."

Robert McAfee Brown (Protestant scholar)

[1]See also: Deut. 17:11, 2 Chron. 17:8-9, Mk. 4:33-34; cf. Neh. 8:7-8, Acts 8:27-31 [2]Eph. 4:4-5 [3]Phil. 1:27 [4]Phil. 2:2 [5]1 Pet. 3:8

The Catholic Church added illegitimate books to the Bible

The early Church denied the canonicity
and inspiration of these seven Apocryphal books,
but the Catholic Church added them centuries later.

THE ONE-MINUTE APOLOGIST SAYS:

*It was Protestantism that removed these "deuterocanonical"
books from the Bible, many centuries later. And contrary to the
myth, the early Church did indeed accept those books as Scripture.*

The seven disputed books are: Tobit, Judith, 1 and 2 Maccabees, Wisdom of Solomon, Ecclesiasticus (or Sirach), and Baruch. Catholic Bibles also include an additional six chapters (107 verses) in Esther and three chapters (174 verses) in Daniel.

According to major Protestant scholars and historians (see bibliography on the next page), in the first four centuries Church leaders (e.g., St. Justin Martyr, Tertullian, St. Augustine, St. Ambrose, St. Cyprian, St. Irenaeus) generally recognized these seven books as canonical and scriptural, following the Septuagint Greek translation of the Old Testament, following the council of Rome (382), and general consensus, finalized the New Testament canon while also including the deuterocanon, in lists that were identical to that of the Council of Trent (1545-1563).

There's a scholarly consensus that this canon was pretty much accepted from the fourth century to the sixteenth, and indeed, the earliest Greek manuscripts of the Old Testament: the Codex Sinaiticus (fourth century) and Codex Alexandrinus (c. 450) include the (unseparated) deuterocanonical books. The Dead Sea Scrolls found at Qumran did not contain Esther, but did contain Tobit.

A PROTESTANT MIGHT FURTHER OBJECT:

Yet, St. Jerome, who was the greatest Bible scholar in the early Church, and author of the Latin Vulgate, didn't accept these extra books. We know what books were in the Old Testament from the Jewish synod of Jamnia (c. A.D. 90), which excluded the Apocrypha. The Jews knew very well what books were in their own Bible!

THE ONE-MINUTE APOLOGIST SAYS:

According to Douglas and Geisler, Jamnia was not an authoritative council, but simply a gathering of scholars, and similar events occurred afterward. In fact, at Jamnia the canonicity of books such as Esther, Ecclesiastes, and Song of Solomon was also disputed. Since both Protestants and Catholics accept these books today, this shows that Jamnia did not "settle" anything. The Jews were still arguing about the canonicity of the books mentioned earlier and also Proverbs into the early second century.

And St. Jerome's sometimes critical views on these books are not as clear-cut as Protestants often make them out to be. In his *Apology Against Rufinus* (402) for example, he wrote:

> When I repeat what the Jews say against the Story of Susanna and the Hymn of the Three Children, and the fables of Bel and the Dragon, which are not contained in the Hebrew Bible, the man who makes this a charge against me proves himself to be a fool and a slanderer; for I explained not what I thought but what they commonly say against us (*Apology Against Rufinus,* Book II, 33).

Significantly, St. Jerome included the deuterocanonical books in the Vulgate, his Latin translation of the Bible. (And he defended the inspiration of Judith in a preface to it.) All in all, there is no clear evidence that St. Jerome rejected these seven books, and much to suggest that he accepted them as inspired Scripture, as the Catholic Church does today. But St. Jerome (like any Church father) does not have the final authority in the Church. He's not infallible. The historical evidence, all things considered, strongly supports the Catholic belief that these books are inspired and thus indeed part of Holy Scripture.

✠

"In practice Athanasius appears to have paid little attention to the formal distinction between those books which he listed in the canon and those which were suitable for the instruction of new Christians [Athanasius cited Wisdom of Solomon, Sirach, Esther, Judith, and Tobit]. He was familiar with the text of all, and quoted from them freely, often with the same introductory formulae — 'as it is written,' 'as the scripture says,' etc."

F. F. BRUCE (PROTESTANT BIBLE SCHOLAR)

Bibliography

F. F. Bruce, *The Canon of Scripture.*

F. L. Cross and E.A. Livingstone, editors, *Oxford Dictionary of the Christian Church.*

J. D. Douglas, editor, *The New Bible Dictionary.*

Norman L. Geisler and William E. Nix, *From God to Us: How We Got Our Bible.*

J.N.D. Kelly, *Early Christian Doctrines.*

James Orr, general editor, *The International Standard Bible Encyclopedia.*

Philip Schaff, *History of the Christian Church* and *Post-Nicene Christianity.*

Brooke Foss Westcott, *A General Survey of the History of the Canon of the New Testament.*

We can know which books belong in the Bible simply by reading them

Biblical books are self-attesting; they tell us that they're inspired. Therefore we don't need a church to tell us which books are in the canon of Scripture.

THE ONE-MINUTE APOLOGIST SAYS:
It's true that there are several internal biblical evidences of inspiration and canonicity, yet (despite this fact) there were many significant disputes in the early Church regarding the books of the Bible.

Many now-accepted books were questioned, and many non-biblical books were thought by some to be canonical. This by itself argues strongly against a self-attesting canon.

Furthermore, the internal evidences for inspiration vary greatly in strength. The author of Hebrews doesn't identify himself (nor does the author of 1, 2, or 3 John), and some scholars believe that he denies being an apostle[1] ("attested to us by those who heard him"). The writer of the book of James does not, in his epistle, make the claim to being an apostle, although he most likely was. Jude was questioned because it cited the Book of Enoch[2] and possibly the Assumption of Moses.[3] Only the author of Revelation claims direct inspiration.

But nothing illustrates the falsity of the notion of a "self-attesting" canon better than the history of the process of canonization itself, in which Church authority was needed to establish the canon once and for all. The early Church did not even become aware that there was a canon until the end of the second century. St. Athanasius was the first person to list our present twenty-seven New Testament books, in the year 367: more than 300 years after the death of Jesus. Many other "anomalous" facts indicate the numerous substantial difficulties of canonicity.

It is a historical fact that many biblical books were accepted only very slowly. St. Justin Martyr (d. 165) didn't recognize Philippians or 1 Timothy. The Muratorian Canon (c. 190) excluded Hebrews, James, 1 Peter, and 2 Peter. The Council of Nicaea in 325 questioned the canonicity of James, 2 Peter, 2 John, 3 John, and Jude. Even up to the late fourth century, the book of James had not even been quoted in the West. The books of Hebrews, 2 Peter, 2 and 3 John, and Revelation were also still being disputed at that late date. Revelation was rejected by St. Cyril of Jerusalem (d. 386), St. John Chrysostom (d. 407), and St. Gregory Nazianzen (d. 389). None of this is consistent with the notion that it is easy to determine a biblical book (that is, an inspired book) simply by reading it.

At the same time, we observe that many non-scriptural books (by both Catholic and Protestant reckoning) were regarded as scriptural by many important people and lists of canonical books in the early Church. The Gospels of St. Justin Martyr contained apocryphal materials. The Epistle of Barnabas and the Didache were regarded as Scripture by St. Clement of Alexandria (d.c. 215) and Origen (d.c. 254); so was the Shepherd of Hermas, by St. Irenaeus (d.c. 200), Tertullian (d.c. 225), Origen, and St. Clement of Alexandria. The Muratorian Canon of c. 190 included the Apocalypse of Peter. The well-known Codex Sinaiticus of the late fourth century still included the Epistle of Barnabas and the Shepherd of Hermas.

A Protestant Might Further Object:

All this shows is that Church fathers were fallible men, just like everyone else.

Yet as the Bible came to be studied and understood more over time, men were better able to see which books were truly inspired and which were not — by the clear indications in the books themselves, not by listening to some church authority.

The One-Minute Apologist Says:

It's very easy to make such (somewhat logically circular) claims; hindsight is 20-20. However, there is no way to test them other than by looking at what actually happened in history. Are we to believe that the same people in the early Church who developed doctrines like the Holy Trinity, who were so close in time and space to the Apostles and to Christ Himself, didn't understand which books belonged in the Bible as well as we do today, because they were poor readers, or slow to comprehend the relatively obvious? The fact remains that there were disagreements because some books were not all that clearly inspired, and other non-biblical books seemed to be. We expect men to disagree; all the more need for a guiding authority.

The Church decided on the canon in the councils of Hippo (393) and Carthage (397), both influenced heavily by St. Augustine. It is sometimes objected that these were merely local councils, but they were preceded by a Roman Council (382) of identical opinion, and were ratified by Popes Innocent I (405, 414) and Gelasius I (495). The sixth Council of Carthage (419) also concurred.

All the evidence only confirms what common sense tells us: that the Bible needs an extrabiblical authority to vouch for its content, and that God has provided us with such an authority in the Church.

⊹

"[O]nly one book of the New Testament explicitly claims
prophetic inspiration. . . . It is unlikely, for example, that the
Spirit's witness would enable a reader to discern that
Ecclesiastes is the word of God while Ecclesiasticus is not."

F. F. Bruce (Protestant Bible scholar)

[1]Heb. 2:3 [2]Jude 14-15 [3]Jude 9

Catholics are taught not to read the Bible for themselves

The Catholic Church doesn't want its members to learn that their religion is unbiblical. That's why it used to chain up Bibles in churches and for centuries forbade Bible translations in the vernacular.

THE ONE-MINUTE APOLOGIST SAYS:
This cherished myth of Protestant polemics is simply false.
The Catholic Church highly encourages personal Scripture reading; at the same time it urges the faithful to approach the Bible within the framework of Catholic tradition, and to avoid excessive individualism of interpretation.

It is true that, generally speaking, Protestants read their Bibles considerably more than Catholics do. This is the natural result of emphasizing the Bible as the only infallible source of Christian truth (and thus falling into an equally serious error at the other end of the spectrum: seriously neglecting Church history and Tradition). But it does not follow from this observation that the Catholic Church has ever forbidden or discouraged Bible-reading. The Church's actual teaching on this matter can be easily seen in numerous official statements. For example, seventy years before Vatican II (in 1893), Pope Leo XIII wrote:

> Let all . . . understand how deeply the sacred books should be esteemed, and with what eagerness and reverence they should approach this great arsenal of heavenly arms. . . . As St. Jerome says, "To be ignorant of the Scripture is not to know Christ.". . . . "A man who is well grounded in the testimonies of the Scripture is the bulwark of the Church."[1]

Likewise, in 1943 Pope Pius XII reminded the Church — citing his predecessor Benedict XV — to read Scripture "piously" and "meditate on it constantly," for the Bible is that "by which the spiritual life is nourished unto perfection."[2]

The accusations that the Catholic Church forbade vernacular translations, and chained Bibles in order to keep them from the common people, are historically misinformed. In fact, Bibles were chained in libraries so that they would not be stolen, precisely because they were so valued and treasured (especially before the invention of the movable-type printing press in the mid-fifteenth century), in order to be more accessible to all.

(Protestants were known to do the same thing themselves for some 300 years.) And vernacular Bible translations in fact became very common by the Middle Ages, as Latin ceased to be a language of the people. Scores of Church-approved translations in many European vernacular languages appeared in the late fifteenth century alone. When the Church did oppose certain bad vernacular translations, it was out of a desire to protect the integrity of Scripture — something any Protestant can appreciate.

A PROTESTANT MIGHT FURTHER OBJECT:

Yet the Catholic Church controls the interpretation of the Bible so tightly that it really doesn't matter if Catholics are allowed to read it or not. They are told what to think rather than allowed to learn from the Scriptures themselves. So in the end that is no different from saying that Catholics can't read the Bible at all.

THE ONE-MINUTE APOLOGIST SAYS:

This is also widely believed, but untrue. Scripture is deep and rich in meaning; never has the Catholic Church claimed to provide a prepackaged interpretation of every verse, binding on all believers to accept. In fact, the 1911 *Catholic Encyclopedia* article "Biblical Exegesis" states about "Defined Texts":

> The Catholic commentator is bound to adhere to the interpretation of texts which the Church has defined either expressly or implicitly. The number of these texts is small, so that the commentator can easily avoid any transgression of this principle.

The Council of Trent (1545-1563) listed only seven biblical passages that were not allowed to be interpreted in a certain way: 1) Luke 22:19, 1 Corinthians 11:24 (the Eucharist); 2) John 3:5 (baptism); 3) Matthew 18:18, John 20:22-23 (priesthood); 4) Romans 5:12 (original sin); and 5) James 6:14 (anointing of the sick). Even in those cases, interpretations that did not contradict Catholic dogma were allowed.

Most (if not all) Protestants are subject to similar restrictions. No Calvinist, for example, is allowed to find a verse in the Bible that proves a Christian can apostatize or fall away, or one that suggests God wills universal rather than limited atonement (and there are many such passages). He can't deny total depravity in any text, or irresistible grace (both binding Calvinist dogmas). Contrary to the widespread myth, the Catholic student of Scripture is bound by very little and has virtually as much freedom of inquiry as the Protestant exegete.

✠

"To the possession by worthy lay men of licensed translations the Church was never opposed; but to place such a weapon as an English Bible in the hands of men who had no regard for authority, and who would use it without being instructed how to use it properly, was dangerous not only to the souls of those who read, but to the peace and order of the Church."

JAMES GAIRDNER (PROTESTANT CHURCH HISTORIAN)

[1]*Providentissimus Deus* (On the Study of Holy Scripture)
[2]*Divino Afflante Spiritu* (The Most Opportune Way to Promote Biblical Studies)

The Church

The notion of bishops and a hierarchical Church is unbiblical

Scripture does not teach only one form of Church government. The Catholic hierarchy stands contrary to the egalitarian spirit of the Bible and the early Church.

THE ONE-MINUTE APOLOGIST SAYS:
The Bible provides plenty of support for episcopal government of the Church, which is why the early Church was clearly hierarchical.

In this area, as in many concerning the biblical evidence for Catholicism, the best method is to get out of the way and simply let the Bible speak for itself. Bishops (Greek: *episkopos*) are specifically mentioned in several places, including Acts 1:20 ("office") and Philippians 1:1 ("To all the saints in Christ Jesus who are at Philip'pi, with the bishops and deacons"). Furthermore, we see in Scripture particular duties assigned to men who were regarded as overseers over regions, rather than individual churches: the power to ordain priests or appoint elders,[1] the prerogative to excommunicate, management and administration of church affairs, and a special duty of defending the faith (emphases added):

Acts 20:28: "Take heed to yourselves and to all the flock, in which the Holy Spirit has made you *overseers*, to care for the church of God which He obtained with the blood of His own Son."

1 Timothy 3:1-5: "If any one aspires to the office of *bishop*, he desires a noble task. Now a bishop must be above reproach, the husband of one wife, temperate, sensible, dignified, hospitable, an apt teacher, no drunkard, not violent but gentle, not quarrelsome, and no lover of money. He must manage his own household well, keeping his children submissive and respectful in every way; for if a man does not know how to manage his own household, how can he care for God's church?"

Titus 1:5-9: "This is why I left you in Crete, that you might amend what was defective, and appoint elders in every town. . . . [A] *bishop*, as God's steward, must be blameless . . . he must hold firm to the sure word as taught, so that he may be able to give instruction in sound doctrine and also to confute those who contradict it."

1 Peter 2:25: "For you were straying like sheep, but have now returned to the Shepherd and Guardian [*episkopos*] of your souls."

In that last verse, Jesus Himself is called a "bishop," thus demonstrating the analogy of authority and oversight from God to the Church.

A PROTESTANT MIGHT FURTHER OBJECT:

Sure, the word "bishop" appears in the Bible, but hierarchical distinctions do not.

The Bible teaches that bishops, elders, and deacons are all synonymous terms for the same office: roughly that of a pastor today. It doesn't indicate that bishops are higher than these other offices.

THE ONE-MINUTE APOLOGIST SAYS:

To the contrary, in Titus 1:5 the bishop is higher than an elder because he is charged to "appoint" them "in every town." This suggests both hierarchy and regional administration or jurisdiction. Bishops and deacons are both mentioned in Philippians 1:1, which would be odd if they were synonymous. 1 Timothy 3:1-7 also discusses bishops, then goes on to treat deacons separately in 3:8-10 ("Deacons likewise . . .").

We would expect some overlapping or variability in function of ministers in the early Church, because it was just the beginning of the development of ecclesiology. The doctrine of the Church and its government would take time to develop, just as the Trinitarian and Christological doctrine would for several centuries. Even the Apostle Paul called himself a "minister" or deacon (Greek: *diakonos*) more than once,[2] but no one thinks that is all he was.

We can reasonably conclude, then, that the sometimes-fluid nature of the early Church's government does not overcome the passages about the function and necessity of bishops, or the later history of increasing hierarchical structure in the Church of the first few centuries.

✝

"For the apostolic origin of episcopacy the following points may be made: (1) The position of James, who evidently stood at the head of the church in Jerusalem. . . . (2) The office of the assistants and delegates of the apostles, like Timothy, Titus, Silas, Epaphroditus, Luke, Mark, who had a sort of supervision of several churches and congregational officers. . . . (3) The angels of the seven churches of Asia, who . . . indicate a monarchical shaping of the church government in the days of John. . . . (4) The testimony of Ignatius of Antioch, a disciple of John . . . presupposes the episcopate . . . as already existing. (5) The statement of Clement of Alexandria, that John instituted bishops after his return from Patmos."

PHILIP SCHAFF (PROTESTANT CHURCH HISTORIAN)

[1]Acts 14:23 [2]1 Cor. 3:5, 2 Cor. 3:6, 6:4, Eph. 3:7, Col. 1:23, 25

The Church is the invisible sum total of all true believers

The notion that the "one true Church"
must be a visible institution is a false tradition of men.

THE ONE-MINUTE APOLOGIST SAYS:
*The Bible teaches us that the Church is a visible, identifiable
institution with a verifiable history of unchanging apostolic teaching.*

It is true that Catholics believe in an "invisible" Church in one sense: namely, the Mystical Body of Christ. We hold that all Christians who have been baptized in the name of the Father, Son, and Holy Spirit are part of the Church in that sense, however imperfectly. But from this it doesn't follow that there cannot also be a visible, institutional body of believers whose members can be said properly to belong to Christ's True Church. When Jesus and Scripture speak of the Church, it is usually in terms that suggest a tangible, specific, active presence in the world and in the community of believers:

> **Matthew 5:14-16:** "You are the light of the world. A city set on a hill cannot be hid. Nor do men light a lamp and put it under a bushel, but on a stand, and it gives light to all in the house. Let your light so shine before men, that they may see your good works and give glory to your Father who is in heaven."

> **Matthew 18:15-17:** "If your brother sins against you, go and tell him his fault, between you and him alone. If he listens to you, you have gained your brother. But if he does not listen, take one or two others along with you, that every word may be confirmed by the evidence of two or three witnesses. If he refuses to listen to them, tell it to the church; and if he refuses to listen even to the church, let him be to you as a Gentile and a tax collector."

> **1 Timothy 3:15:** "[T]he household of God, which is the church of the living God, the pillar and bulwark of the truth."[1]

Some Christians seem to think that the Apostle Paul was a kind of "lone ranger," not part of any Church but single-handedly (or with the help of a few friends) preaching and spreading the gospel. The Bible, on the other hand, recounts how Paul was subject to the direction and sanction of the institutional Church. He, too (even though he was an apostle, who wrote much of the New Testament), was under authority:

> **Acts 13:1-4**: "Now in the church at Antioch there were prophets and teachers, Barnabas, Simeon who was called Niger, Lucius of Cyrene, Mana-en a member of the court of Herod the tetrarch, and Saul. While they were worshiping the Lord and fasting, the Holy Spirit said, 'Set apart for me Barnabas and Saul for the work to which I have called them.' Then after fasting and praying they laid their hands on them and sent them off. So, being sent out by the Holy Spirit, they went down to Seleucia; and from there they sailed to Cyprus."[2]

> **Galatians 1:18-19**: "I went up to Jerusalem to visit Cephas, and remained with him fifteen days. But I saw none of the other apostles except James the Lord's brother."

In fact, Paul believed that his apostolic work stemmed directly from the authoritative commission he received from the hierarchy:

> **Galatians 2:9**: "[A]nd when they perceived the grace that was given to me, James and Cephas [Peter] and John, who were reputed to be pillars, gave to me and Barnabas the right hand of fellowship, that we should go to the Gentiles and they to the circumcised."

A Protestant Might Further Object:

But the words of Jesus Himself suggest that the Church is first and foremost invisible, not bound by denominational structures. For example, doesn't His analogy of the sheep and the shepherd,[3] who know each other, show that the Church is a mystical, invisible body consisting of the elect and truly saved only?

The One-Minute Apologist Says:

No, because Scripture also describes the unsaved reprobate as "sheep,"[4] refers to sheep that have "gone astray,"[5] and applies the description to the nation of Israel,[6] and indeed, all men.[7] The overall biblical theme concerning "sheep" refers to the sense that all men, and particularly Israel, are God's children. But this doesn't preclude the existence of a visible, institutional Church — especially since the latter is clearly indicated in the Bible.

✠

"But because it is now our intention to discuss the visible church, let us learn even from the simple title 'mother' how useful, indeed how necessary, it is that we should know her. For there is no other way to enter into life unless this mother conceive us in her womb, give us birth, nourish us at her breast, and lastly, unless she keep us under her care and guidance until, putting off mortal flesh, we become like the angels."

JOHN CALVIN

[1]cf. Matt. 16:18 [2]cf. 14:26-28 [3]Jn. 10:1-16; cf. 2 Tim. 2:19, 1 Jn. 2:19
[4]Ps. 74:1 [5]Ps. 119:176 [6]Ezek. 34:2-3, 13, 23, 30 [7]Is. 53:6

Catholicism is a half-pagan religion, blending non-Christian beliefs and practices with the gospel

How could true Christianity pollute the teachings of Jesus with pagan images, rituals, and ideas?

THE ONE-MINUTE APOLOGIST SAYS:
Truth is truth wherever it is found. The Catholic Church, following St. Paul's example, makes use of existing practices to spread Christ's message.

All of God's creation is good. An act or practice (not including those that are immoral, like cannibalism or human sacrifice) can be good or evil depending on the circumstances and meaning given to it. During the fourth century, many items or gestures from pagan rituals were indeed blended into the Christian faith: such as genuflection, incense, and candles. But there is nothing intrinsically wrong with such things; even if they were part of pre-Christian worship, their incorporation into Christian practice does not necessarily constitute a pagan "pollution" of Christianity.

In fact, by adopting pre-Christian elements and practices — devised by men in an attempt to reach God without the benefit of revelation — the Church can "reclaim" them for Christ, directing them toward the worship of the true God. For example, the pagans of northern Europe (like the ancient enemies of the Hebrews) used trees as idols. We use the evergreen Christmas tree as a symbol of everlasting life: life in the dead of winter, just as Christ brought life to the deadness of humanity. The tree itself is a neutral (and beautiful) object: a part of God's good creation. The key to true worship is the inner attitude; the heart.[1]

Some object that the word "Easter" is of pagan origin; hence many non-Catholic Christians prefer the term "Resurrection Day." Now, the etymological derivation of the word is uncertain, but some think it came from the Anglo-Saxon spring goddess, Eostre. If so, using the word to signify Christ's Resurrection would represent another Christianization or "baptizing" of a human custom in order to supersede the old paganism and give the rituals an entirely new meaning in the light of Christ's revelation. A word is not evil in and of itself. Even sacred words usually have secular origins.

A PROTESTANT MIGHT FURTHER OBJECT:
That may be all well and good, as far as it goes. But there is still no scriptural warrant for such practices of "incorporation." Christianity must always be based on the Bible — not paganism — because that is God's revelation to and for us: our standard

or guidebook as to what is right and wrong in practice and belief. This rules out things like Mary-worship, which came from the ancient Egyptian worship of the goddess Isis.

THE ONE-MINUTE APOLOGIST SAYS:

The Bible does contain indications of this practice, such as the Apostle Paul's speech to the Greek intellectuals and philosophers at the Areopagus, or Mars Hill, in Athens. Here, in Acts 17:15-34, he effectively evangelized by using symbols and ideas familiar to his hearers. He complimented their religiosity and noted a pagan "altar" (an idol!) with the inscription, "To an unknown god." He then preached that the "unknown god" was Yahweh, the God of the Jews: the true God, as opposed to "shrines made by man," and the sovereign and sustaining creator. He quoted pagan poets and philosophers — Epimenides of Crete (also cited in Titus 1:12) and Aratus of Cilicia — and expanded upon their understanding.

When the Church annexes pagan customs and holy days such as Easter, Christmas, All Souls Day, and All Saints Day, it is simply utilizing St. Paul's evangelization strategy. This does not represent a wholesale adoption of paganism, or some diabolical mixture of idolatry and paganism with Christianity. If that were true, Paul would also stand guilty. Yet he states with confidence:

> **1 Corinthians 9:19-22:** "For though I am free from all men, I have made myself a slave to all, that I might win the more. To the Jews I became as a Jew, in order to win Jews; to those under the law I became as one under the law — though not being myself under the law — that I might win those under the law. To those outside the law I became as one outside the law — not being without law toward God but under the law of Christ — that I might win those outside the law. To the weak I became weak, that I might win the weak. I have become all things to all men, that I might by all means save some."

Interestingly, this critique can backfire on Protestants, for skeptics make a similar criticism of Christianity itself: tracing the doctrine of the Trinity to Babylonian three-headed gods, for example, and Christ and His Resurrection to Mithraism or one of many other "God-hero myths." But these pagan associations (or curious similarities) don't stop Protestant critics of the Catholic Church from believing in the Triune God or the Resurrection. Neither do the superficial similarities between Marian veneration and Isis-worship stop Catholics from properly honoring the mother of their savior.

✝

"[T]here lurked in those pagan festivals themselves, in spite of all their sensual abuses, a deep meaning and an adaptation to a real want; they might be called unconscious prophecies of the Christmas feast . . . the Sun of righteousness, the Light of the world . . . on the twenty-fifth of December, after the winter solstice, breaks the growing power of darkness, and begins anew his heroic career."

PHILIP SCHAFF (PROTESTANT CHURCH HISTORIAN)

[1]See, for example, Mk. 7:6-8

Miracles and the supernatural gifts ceased after the death of the Apostles

The Bible teaches that "when the perfect comes, the imperfect will pass away." Thus the Catholic Church cannot claim that its ministers today enjoy the gifts and authority that Christ gave to the Apostles.

THE ONE-MINUTE APOLOGIST SAYS:
The idea that spiritual gifts or charisms, or even offices in the Church, were intended for the apostolic age only and not for all times is not taught in the Bible; and furthermore it makes little sense. God gave His gifts to the Church so that it could better fulfill its mission, which continued after the apostolic age.

Some Protestants (called "dispensationalists") hold that God operates in different ways according to particular ages. A disbelief in miracles and supernatural gifts can also be the result of an anti-supernaturalist or skeptical bent. But the most common argument from Evangelicals in this regard stems from 1 Corinthians 13:8-11. They view the passage, which speaks of supernatural gifts "passing away," as proof that whatever charisms the apostolic Church may have received from God, these did not carry on through the ages. Certainly the Catholic Church cannot lay claim to them today.

But this is very poor exegesis. The context makes clear that Paul is referring to the next life as the "perfect," since in 13:12 he states: "For now we see in a mirror dimly, but then face to face. Now I know in part; then I shall understand fully, even as I have been fully understood."[1] In other words, the gifts that are part of earthly faith and ministry will not be necessary in heaven.

Those who are known as "cessationists" claim that the "perfect" referred to by Paul is the Bible; but this is merely a preconceived notion imposed onto the text. And why would God remove the blessings for the roles which He had foreordained each of us to play?

Moreover, if these gifts were to cease, why would Paul spend the better part of three chapters (1 Cor. 12-14) defining and elaborating upon them for use in the Church? He urges the Corinthians to "earnestly desire the spiritual gifts"[2] and to "earnestly desire the higher gifts."[3] Paul would have been wasting his time if he knew these gifts were about to pass away.

A Protestant Might Further Object:

These gifts were intended only for the earliest period in Christian history, to attest to the gospel and the life, death, and Resurrection of Jesus Christ.

But after that they were not strictly necessary. That goes for offices within the Church, too — so-called "apostolic succession." Catholics are going beyond the Bible at this point and are simply trying to justify their man-made inventions and traditions.

The One-Minute Apologist Says:

In this passage St. Paul uses typical Hebrew rhetoric: an exaggerated form of "comparison and contrast." He means to convey the idea that even important things such as prophecy and knowledge will count for little compared with the glory of being in the presence of God ("face-to-face"). They are not to be sources of pride.

In the surrounding context, Paul casually assumes that gifts would be present in the Church. He writes about "varieties of gifts,"[4] details their distribution by the Holy Spirit ("To each is given the manifestation of the Spirit . . . one and the same Spirit, who apportions to each one individually as he wills"),[5] shows that different Christians have different roles and charisms ("Are all teachers? Do all work miracles?"),[6] and in chapter 14 provides a detailed exposition of the use of tongues and prophecy in the Church. Nowhere does he ever indicate that this is only a temporary state of affairs.

As for apostolic succession, that has clear biblical warrant, too. It is shown, for example, that the apostles (not Jesus) selected Matthias as the successor of Judas.[7] Judas was called a "bishop" (*episkopos*) in the same passage (1:20), where the Bible specifically describes a process of succession: "For it is written in the book of Psalms . . . 'His office let another take'" (cf. 1:25: "to take the place in this ministry and apostleship from which Judas turned aside"). If apostles can be replaced in this fashion, and if one was called a bishop, then by logical extension there could be an unbroken apostolic succession of bishops, as the successors of the Apostles.

This conception is present, whole and entire, in the Bible. In fact, in 1 Corinthians 12, St. Paul seems to casually assume that the office of apostle was an ongoing one in the Church. The biblical and historical office of bishop would account for this. The Bible contains all the evidence that one would expect to find in favor of a continuance of all the spiritual gifts, including Church offices.

✠

"1 Corinthians 13:1-13 is obviously directed against a kind of enthusiasm,
where zeal for the more spectacular charismata, particularly prophecy,
glossalalia and knowledge, had provoked jealousy, arrogance, irritability, and
kindred sins. Love had been the loser, and love provides the test (13:4-7).
No matter how outstanding the gifts exercised, if they produced
a loveless character, Paul counts them of no value whatsoever."

James D.G. Dunn (Protestant New Testament scholar)

---

[1] cf. 1 Jn. 3:2, Rev. 22:4 [2]1Cor. 13:1 [3]1 Cor. 12:31; cf. 14:39; 1 Thess. 5:19-21
[4]1 Cor. 12:4 [5]1 Cor. 12:7-11 [6]1 Cor. 12:27-31 [7]Acts 1:20-26

The Catholic Church believes it can damn people to hell by excommunication

This proves that it sets itself higher than God. For who but God Himself has the power of final judgment?

THE ONE-MINUTE APOLOGIST SAYS:
The term "excommunication" means, literally, "out of communion" with the Church — not damnation to hell. The Catholic Church doesn't even say with certainty that any particular person is in hell, much less claim to possess the power to put people there.

Excommunication is a formal declaration that a Catholic is "outside the Church"; because such a person has egregiously diverged from its doctrines, he is excluded from the sacraments and from the Christian fellowship of believers. The purpose of such an exclusion is not to punish the sinner but to encourage him to repent; the goal is restoration, not damnation. It's true that we hold that no one can be saved outside the Church, having finally and deliberately disobeyed it despite knowing that it speaks truth, but this is not fundamentally different from Protestants' saying "a person will not be saved if he does not accept Christ as his Lord and Savior," or the Bible stating that "fornicators will not inherit the Kingdom of God." Scripture does not damn people to hell and neither does excommunication; both merely state the way things are.

The Church has no power to condemn anyone to hell (that is solely God's prerogative). But it does have the power to exclude people from communion with itself, for the purpose of ultimately reclaiming their souls. Excommunication is perfectly in line with biblical practices and teachings, as seen in the following passages:

1 Corinthians 5:3-5: "For though absent in body I am present in spirit, and as if present, I have already pronounced judgment in the name of the Lord Jesus on the man who has done such a thing. When you are assembled, and my spirit is present, with the power of our Lord Jesus, you are to deliver this man to Satan for the destruction of the flesh, that his spirit may be saved in the day of the Lord Jesus."[1]

2 Thessalonians 3:6: "Now we command you, brethren, in the name of our Lord Jesus Christ, that you keep away from any brother who is living in idleness and not in accord with the tradition that you received from us."[2]

1 Timothy 1:18-20: "[W]age the good warfare, holding faith and a good conscience. By rejecting conscience, certain persons have made shipwreck of their faith, among them Hymenae'us and Alexander, whom I have delivered to Satan that they may learn not to blaspheme."[3]

A PROTESTANT MIGHT FURTHER OBJECT:

But even if that were true, what about the Catholic Church's practice of "anathematizing" people? At times, such as in the Council of Trent, the Church has declared of certain people, *anathema sit*, a term that means, "Let him be accursed."

THE ONE-MINUTE APOLOGIST SAYS:

The vivid Greek term *anathema*, which indeed means "accursed," is directed by the Council of Trent and other Catholic ecumenical councils primarily toward doctrines, rather than persons, based on the ancient practice in the Church of condemning false teachings. The word and concept are found in biblical passages such as the following:

1 Corinthians 16:22: "If any one has no love for the Lord, let him be accursed. Our Lord, come!"

Galatians 1:8: "But even if we, or an angel from heaven, should preach to you a gospel contrary to that which we preached to you, let him be accursed."

It is not improper at all to define correct doctrine and reject false doctrines. St. Paul does this constantly. Since it is a biblical and Pauline practice, the Catholic Church has aligned itself (as always) with what is revealed in the Bible. Occasionally in a Church council, an individual is condemned by name, but such cases still do not mean that the Catholic Church believes he is necessarily damned, per the above reasoning. It all boils down to what these words mean and how they were intended.

Neither excommunication nor anathemas imply the Church's condemning anyone to hell. Excommunication is a Church law, excluding a notorious sinner from the communion of the faithful.[4] Its purpose is to warn the sinner of the danger he runs of incurring eternal ruin, unless he repent of his sin. The "delivering of the sinner to Satan," which we find in the Roman Pontifical, is based on the words of St. Paul, who delivered the incestuous sinner to Satan, "that his spirit might be saved in the Day of the Lord Jesus Christ."[5]

✠

"When St. Paul said, 'Let him be anathema' who preaches an heretical gospel, he did not condemn the heretic to hell, but stigmatized the willful teacher of false doctrines as a rebel against the Gospel of Christ. The Church, in the anathemas which accompany the canons of her Councils, merely imitates the example of the Apostle."

BERTRAND CONWAY

[1]cf. Rom. 16:17, Titus 3:9-11 [2]cf. Mt. 18:17-18 [3]cf. 2 Tim. 2:14-19, 4:14-15 [4]Canons 2257-2267 [5]1 Cor. 5:5; cf. 1 Tim. 1:20

The Church can contain only the holy and saved

Christ's Church cannot contain rank sinners within it. Otherwise, today's Christians would be no better than the hypocritical Pharisees.

THE ONE-MINUTE APOLOGIST SAYS:
The Bible teaches us to let the "wheat" and the "tares" (or "weeds") grow together in the Church,[1] rather than immediately kick out everyone who is a sinner.

Holy Scripture contains an abundant amount of proof against the puritanical notion that sinners can never be counted part of Christ's Church. When Jesus talked about the "kingdom of heaven," He said that it would include sinners as well as the righteous, until the Last Day. He compared the kingdom of heaven to a wedding feast, at which are gathered "both bad and good; so the wedding hall was filled with guests."[2] Elsewhere He used a fishing analogy:

> **Matthew 13:47-49**: "Again, the kingdom of heaven is like a net which was thrown into the sea and gathered fish of every kind; when it was full, men drew it ashore and sat down and sorted the good into vessels but threw away the bad. So it will be at the close of the age. The angels will come out and separate the evil from the righteous."

Note that in these parables, the evil and the sinners were not separated from the righteous until Judgment Day.

St. Paul called the assembly at Corinth, for example, the "church of God,"[3] yet seriously rebuked it for immorality that surpassed that of the pagans.[4] He says that they are "still of the flesh" because of rampant "jealousy and strife"[5] and rebukes their tendency to receive "a different gospel," even "another Jesus" from the one they had accepted.[6] Yet despite their serious sinfulness and divisions, they are nonetheless part of Christ's Church.

We observe the same dynamic with regard to the seven churches of Revelation, which throughout chapters two and three are still referred to as "churches" even though they are "wretched, pitiable, poor, blind, and naked,"[7] and are sternly rebuked for a multitude of sins, including idolatry and immorality.

The Galatians (given the titles of "churches" in v. 1:2) scarcely fare any better: "O foolish Galatians! Who has bewitched you? . . . Are you so foolish? Having begun with the Spirit, are you now ending with the flesh?"[8] "But now that you have come to know God, or rather to be known by God, how can you turn back again to the weak and beggarly elemental spirits, whose slaves you want to be once more?"[9]

A PROTESTANT MIGHT FURTHER OBJECT:

But the Bible teaches that Christians should be "perfect." It also says that "no one born of God commits sin; for God's nature abides in him," and that church leaders should be "above reproach." So how can we also believe that unrepentant sinners are still part of the Body of Christ?

THE ONE-MINUTE APOLOGIST SAYS:

Of course the goal of Christian teaching is righteousness and holiness, but it does not follow that every Christian will attain the goal. We are justified by Christ, but that does not mean we immediately cease to sin. Protestants understand this theological distinction (in fact, in their theology they formally separate justification from sanctification, unlike Catholics), so it is surprising that they still often raise these objections.

Jesus knew that sinners could still be believers, and believers sinners, since He taught about the wheat and the tares and the kingdom of God as a fish net that included both "good" and "bad." But these striking passages even go beyond that: the fact that the tares are burned (Matthew 13:40-42 makes it very clear that this represents hell) absolutely proves that within the Church there are not only saved sinners who are justified but insufficiently sanctified, but also people who will eventually be damned.

It's true that holiness is a mark of Christians and thus of Christ's Church. 1 John expresses this idea using proverbial or idealized language. Yet in the same epistle, John also states, "If we say we have no sin, we deceive ourselves" and takes it for granted that we will "confess our sins."[10] This motif is expressed again in a striking passage:

> **1 John 2:1-2:** "My little children, I am writing this to you so that you may not sin; but if any one does sin, we have an advocate with the Father, Jesus Christ the righteous; and He is the expiation for our sins, and not for ours only but also for the sins of the whole world."

Here the presence of sin among believers is casually assumed. James 5:16 likewise urges Christians to "confess your sins to one another," and St. Paul describes himself as "the foremost of sinners";[11] note that this is in the present tense, not past. The notion of the completely, literally "holy" Church on earth, is, then, soundly refuted from abundant biblical evidence to the contrary.

✣

"That the holiest church should produce the greatest sinners is but the natural application of the principle that the corruption of the best is the worst."

RONALD KNOX

[1]Mt. 13:24-30 [2]Mt. 22:10; see 22:1-14 [3]1 Cor. 1:2, 2 Cor. 1:1, cf. 2 Cor. 11:2 [4]1 Cor. 5:1 [5]1 Cor. 3:3 [6]2 Cor. 11:4 [7]Rev. 3:17 [8]Gal. 3:1, 3 [9]Gal. 4:9 [10]1:8-10 [11]1 Tim. 1:15

Denominationalism is not condemned in Scripture

Paul allowed disagreement on secondary doctrines — the minor issues over which today's denominations disagree.

THE ONE-MINUTE APOLOGIST SAYS:
Virtually nothing is more strongly and repeatedly condemned in the Bible than divisions, sectarianism, and denominationalism. The Bible teaches that there is one Church only, with one truth and one unified apostolic tradition.

Doctrinal disunity of any sort is absolutely at odds with biblical teaching, which repeatedly urges unity and forbids divisions of any kind among Christians. At the Last Supper our Lord Jesus prayed for Christians to be "one even as we [the Father and the son] are one" and "perfectly one";[1] He also spoke of the Church as being "one flock" with "one shepherd."[2] St. Luke described the earliest Christians as being "of one heart and soul."[3] St. Peter warned about "false teachers" among Christians, who would "secretly bring in destructive heresies," which go against "the way of truth."[4]

St. Paul, above all, repeatedly condemns "dissensions" and "difficulties,"[5] "quarreling,"[6] "jealousy and strife,"[7] "divisions" and "factions,"[8] and "party spirit,"[9] and calls for Christians to be "united in the same mind and the same judgment."[10] He expressly condemns party affiliations associated with persons, asking rhetorically, "Is Christ divided?"[11] His strong teaching on this topic is aptly summed up in these two passages:

> **1 Timothy 6:3-5**: "If any one teaches otherwise and does not agree with the sound words of our Lord Jesus Christ and the teaching which accords with godliness, he is puffed up with conceit, he knows nothing; he has a morbid craving for controversy and for disputes about words, which produce envy, dissension, slander, base suspicions, and wrangling among men who are depraved in mind and bereft of the truth, imagining that godliness is a means of gain."

> **Titus 3:9-11**: "But avoid stupid controversies, genealogies, dissensions, and quarrels over the law, for they are unprofitable and futile. As for a man who is factious, after admonishing him once or twice, have nothing more to do with him, knowing that such a person is perverted and sinful; he is self-condemned."

A Protestant Might Further Object:

But the entirety of Romans 14 teaches that Christians can disagree with each other!

In it Paul writes, "Let everyone be fully convinced in his own mind." Doesn't this suggest that Christians are allowed a wide latitude in what they can believe, provided they agree on the most important, fundamental doctrines? There are central, primary, essential doctrines, and others that are optional and secondary.

The One-Minute Apologist Says:

Romans 14 isn't a proof text for doctrinal diversity because it has nothing to do with doctrine in the first place, but rather matters of *practice*: such as what is proper to eat ("Let not him who eats despise him who abstains"; "For the kingdom of God is not food and drink"[12]) and esteeming "one day as better than another."[13]

As to the general notion of "central" versus "secondary" doctrines, this is an unbiblical distinction. Jesus urged us to "observe all that I have commanded you,"[14] without distinguishing between lesser and greater teachings. Likewise, St. Paul regards Christian Tradition as of one piece; not an amalgam of permissible competing theories. He writes of "the tradition that you received from us,"[15] "the truth which has been entrusted to you by the Holy Spirit"[16] and "the doctrine which you have been taught."[17] He urges Christians to be "in full accord and of one mind" (Phil. 2:2) and to "stand firm in one spirit, with one mind striving side by side for the faith of the gospel."[18] As Jesus did, he connects doctrinal unity with the one God: "There is one body and one Spirit . . . one Lord, one faith, one baptism."[19]

St. Peter also refers to one, unified "way of righteousness" and "the holy commandment delivered to them,"[20] while St. Jude urges us to "contend for the faith which was once for all delivered to the saints."[21] And Luke 2:42 casually mentions "the Apostles' teaching" without any hint that there were competing interpretations or variations of it. Denominations and all that they entail (particularly, doctrinal contradiction or any sort of theological relativism) are thus clearly ruled out by Scripture.

✟

"Denominationalism thus represents the moral failure of Christianity. And unless the ethics of brotherhood can gain the victory over this divisiveness within the body of Christ it is useless to expect it to be victorious in the world. But before the church can hope to overcome its fatal division it must learn to recognize and to acknowledge the secular character of its denominationalism."

H. Richard Niebuhr (Protestant theologian)

[1]Jn. 17:22-23 [2]Jn. 10:16 [3]Acts 4:32 [4]2 Pet. 2:1-2 [5]Rom. 16:17 [6]Rom. 16:17 [7]1 Cor. 3:3 [8]1 Cor. 11:18-19 [9]Gal. 5:20 [10]1 Cor. 1:10; cf. Phil. 2:2 [11]1 Cor. 1:12-13; cf. 3:4-7 [12]14:2-3, 14-17 [13]14:5 [14]Mt. 28:19 [15]2 Thess. 3:6 [16]2 Tim. 1:14 [17]Rom. 16:17 [18]Phil. 1:27 [19]Eph. 4:3-5 [20]2 Pet. 2:21 [21]Jude 3

The Galileo incident proves that the Catholic Church isn't infallible

It also shows that Catholicism opposes science and scientific open-mindedness.

THE ONE-MINUTE APOLOGIST SAYS:

One Church tribunal's proclamations about Galileo do not overthrow the doctrine of infallibility; nor — once the facts of the matter are properly understood — do they show the Catholic Church to be opposed to science.

The popular story of the Catholic Church's censure of the astronomer Galileo (1564-1642) in 1616 and 1633, supposedly for his rejection of a geocentric universe, may be the most notorious and famous anti-Catholic myth of them all — especially for those who believe religion and science are inexorably opposed.

But the truth of the matter is that Catholic dogma had never enshrined geocentrism, and Galileo (a faithful Catholic) had been supported in his scientific work by many notable churchmen, including three popes. Indeed, his biographer Giorgio de Santillana stated that "It has been known for a long time that a major part of the church intellectuals were on the side of Galileo, while the clearest opposition to him came from secular ideas."[1]

Problems arose when the scientist, although basically correct, became overconfident and obstinate in proclaiming his scientific theory as absolute truth — over and above even Scripture. Accordingly, St. Robert Bellarmine, who was directly involved in the controversy, made it clear that although heliocentrism (a sun-centered universe or solar system) was not irreversibly condemned, a not-yet-proven theory could not be called an unassailable fact.

In 1633 the Church tribunal condemned Galileo's "false opinion of the motion of the Earth and the stability of the Sun" as "contrary to divine Scripture," as well as the notions that "the Sun is the center of the world and does not move from east to west and that the Earth moves and is not the center of the world."

Obviously this was incorrect science. Yet in fairness to the Church it should be noted that Galileo was scientifically fallible, too (Bellarmine certainly had the superior understanding of the nature of a scientific hypothesis). He held that the entire universe revolved around the sun in circular (not elliptical) orbits, and that tides were caused by the rotation of the earth. True heliocentrism wasn't conclusively proven until some 200 years later. In recent times Pope John Paul II famously apologized for the Church's embarrassing mistake, but the Holy Office had in fact already done so — in 1825; and Galileo's written works had been permitted since 1741.

Far more embarrassing and numerous "Bible versus Science" fiascoes in the Protestant world are not nearly as well-known. Martin Luther called Copernicus an "upstart astrologer" in 1539, appealing to Joshua 10:13 as proof that the sun moves around the earth. John Calvin "proved" geocentrism from Psalm 93:1 and contended that belief in a rotating earth would "pervert the order of nature." The Protestant University of Tubingen condemned the heliocentrism of Lutheran astronomer Johann Kepler (1571-1630), not long before the Galileo incident. The Lutheran philosopher Leibnitz (1646-1716) attacked Newton's theory of gravitation. On the other hand, Catholic philosophers such as Nicholas Oresme (c. 1325-1382) and Nicholas of Cusa (1401-1464) had long posited a moving earth, and the sphericity of the earth had been taught even earlier by St. Albert the Great, St. Thomas Aquinas, and Dante.

In any event, the Galileo affair does not threaten the Catholic doctrine of infallibility, because the Church doesn't claim that tribunals possess that gift; only that popes, and ecumenical councils in agreement with them, do. The Catholic faithful were not bound to hold the tribunal's opinion as an article of faith, since it had nothing to do with faith or morals. (The First Vatican Council in 1870 would clarify the longstanding Catholic belief that these were the sole subjects of infallible declarations.)

A Protestant Might Further Object:

But wasn't Galileo also imprisoned and tortured by the Inquisition, in order to force him to recant his theory? Even if it wasn't pretending to act "infallibly" in this case, these cannot be the actions of Christ's Church.

The One-Minute Apologist Says:

In 1633 Galileo was "incarcerated" in the palace of one Niccolini, the ambassador to the Vatican from Tuscany, who admired Galileo. He spent five months with Archbishop Piccolomini in Siena, and then lived in comfortable environments with friends for the rest of his life (although technically under "house arrest"). No evidence exists to prove that he was ever subjected to torture or even discomfort until his death nine years later. Nor is there any evidence, as another myth goes, that he was deliberately blinded (he lost his sight naturally in 1637). Stories of Galileo's "torture" are myths invented and proliferated by a strange alliance of (anti-Catholic) fundamentalists and (anti-religion) skeptics.

"[I]t was a churchman, Nicholas Copernicus, who first advanced the contrary doctrine that the sun and not the earth is the center of our system, round which our planet revolves, rotating on its own axis. . . . Neither Paul III, nor any of the nine popes who followed him, nor the Roman Congregations raised any alarm."

The Catholic Encyclopedia, "Galileo"

---

[1] *The Crime of Galileo* (University of Chicago Press, 1955), xii-xiii

The Papacy

The Bible doesn't teach that the Church had one leader

That was simply a Catholic myth to increase the influence of the papacy and solidify the Church's power.

THE ONE-MINUTE APOLOGIST SAYS:
In fact, the Bible is filled with indications that St. Peter was the leader of the Apostles and of the early Church. In many ways Scripture seems to presume — almost casually — that he was preeminent.

The cumulative effect of many such indications is decisive. Peter alone is given a new name by Jesus (he was formerly named Simon), and in Matthew 16:18 is made the central figure upon whom Jesus will build His Church: "And I tell you, you are Peter ['Rock'], and on this rock I will build my church." Peter alone is given the "keys of the kingdom of heaven"[1] — a symbol of stewardship and supervisory capacity over the house of God, or the Church.

Jesus clearly regarded Peter as a sort of "chief shepherd" of the Christian flock, charged with carrying on His own pastoral office after He was gone. We see that Jesus exhorted *Peter* to feed his sheep;[2] He prayed that *Peter's* faith would be strong so he could in turn strengthen the other apostles.[3] Peter is later observed performing this very role in his exhortation of bishops and elders with a sort of "encyclical" letter.[4] Peter's name invariably appears first in lists of Apostles, and he is even called the "first" in Matthew 10:2.

Peter is regarded as the leader of the Apostles by an angel;[5] another angel tells Cornelius to ask Peter for Christian instruction.[6] Peter authoritatively interprets prophecy,[7] works the first miracle after Pentecost,[8] utters the first anathema,[9] is the first to rebuke and refute doctrinal heresy or error,[10] and offers the sole recorded interpretation of the events on the day of Pentecost, making him the first Christian to preach the gospel in the new Church Age.[11] This speech includes authoritative interpretations of Scripture and doctrinal and disciplinary decisions. He was the first to preach about repentance and baptism,[12] led the first mass baptism,[13] and enjoined the first baptism of Gentiles.[14]

The entire Church appeared to pray for Peter after he was put in prison.[15] He was — following instruction by a revelation — the first Jewish Christian to receive Gentiles into equal fellowship,[16] and was the first traveling missionary and visitor of new churches, even before Paul,[17] and (along with James and John), commissioned St. Paul to evangelize the Gentiles.[18]

A PROTESTANT MIGHT FURTHER OBJECT:

It's true that Peter was an important figure in the early Church. But Paul was even more important.

Paul was the primary missionary of the new Church, and wrote much of the New Testament. Yet no one claims that this is proof of Pauline primacy.

THE ONE-MINUTE APOLOGIST SAYS:

But we're looking in the Bible for evidence of ecclesiastical authority, not importance or influence or even holiness.

Paul had more far-reaching influence, it's true — especially theologically and in the long-term impact of his missions. His supreme greatness as an evangelist is indisputable. And yet in 2 Peter 3:14-16, Peter is presented in Scripture as a man who has so much authority that he can correct those who distort the true meaning of the letters of Paul:

> So also our beloved brother Paul wrote to you according to the wisdom given him, speaking of this as he does in all his letters. There are some things in them hard to understand, which the ignorant and unstable twist to their own destruction, as they do the other scriptures.

Finally, at the only Church council recorded in Scripture — the Jerusalem Council of Acts 15 — it was Peter who presided. Not James (the bishop of Jerusalem), or the great evangelist Paul. Scripture presents Peter to us as the head of the Apostles. To this day the Catholic Church has simply followed that biblical model.

✠

"It was Peter who became the focal point of unity in the great Church, since Peter was probably in fact and effect the bridge-man who did more than any other to hold together the diversity of first-century Christianity. James and Paul, the two other most prominent leading figures in first-century Christianity, were too much identified with their respective 'brands' of Christianity, at least in the eyes of Christians at the opposite end of this particular spectrum. . . . [N]one of them, including none of the rest of the twelve, seem to have played any role of continuing significance for the whole sweep of Christianity."

JAMES D.G. DUNN (PROTESTANT BIBLE SCHOLAR)

[1]Mt. 16:19 [2]Jn. 21:15-17 [3]Lk. 22:32 [4]1 Pet. 5:1 [5]Mk. 16:7 [6]2 Pet. 1:16-21
[7]Acts 10:1-6 [8]Acts 3:6-12; cf. 5:15, 9:40 [9]Acts 5:2-11 [10]Acts 8:14-24
[11]Acts 2:14-41 [12]Acts 2:38 [13]Acts 2:41 [14]Acts 10:44-48 [15]Acts 12:5
[16]Acts 10:9-48 [17]Acts 9:32-38, 43 [18]Gal. 2:9

Jesus did not make Peter the leader of the Apostles

Rather, He conferred power and authority on all of them. At most, all we can say is that Peter is "first among equals."

THE ONE-MINUTE APOLOGIST SAYS:
The "keys of the kingdom of heaven," which Peter receives from Jesus in Matthew 16:19, signifies a singular degree of authority.

Peter alone was given these "keys," signifying that Jesus meant for him to be the leader of the early Church: a primitive version of the office of the papacy. Most commentators agree that the background of the phrase in Hebrew culture is shown in Isaiah 22:20-22,[1] and that Peter was regarded by Jesus as a sort of steward, which in the Old Testament referred to a man "over a house."[2] This was the same office Joseph occupied in Egypt:

> **Genesis 41:39-41,43-44:** "So Pharaoh said to Joseph, 'Since God has shown you all this, there is none so discreet and wise as you are; you shall be over my house, and all my people shall order themselves as you command; only as regards the throne will I be greater than you.' And Pharaoh said to Joseph, 'Behold, I have set you over all the land of Egypt.' . . . Thus he set him over all the land of Egypt. Moreover Pharaoh said to Joseph, 'I am Pharaoh, and without your consent no man shall lift up hand or foot in all the land of Egypt'" (cf. 45:8-9).

Catholics are not alone in their belief that possession of the "keys of the kingdom" gave Peter unique authority among the apostles and in the early Church. Many Protestant Bible scholars have concluded the same thing about Peter's position. For example, noted commentator R.T. France wrote that Peter's role "involves a daunting degree of authority" and that he "controls admission to the house, as the steward, who regulates its administration."[3] The great Protestant biblical scholar F.F. Bruce makes an even stronger declaration about Peter's authority: "About 700 BC an oracle from God announced that this authority in the royal palace in Jerusalem was to be conferred on a man called Eliakim . . . (Isa. 22:22). So in the new community which Jesus was about to build, Peter would be, so to speak, chief steward."[4]

Oscar Cullmann concurs: "Just as in Isaiah 22:22 the Lord puts the keys of the house of David on the shoulders of his servant Eliakim, so does Jesus hand over to

Peter the keys of the house of the kingdom of heaven and by the same stroke establishes him as his superintendent."[5]

A PROTESTANT MIGHT FURTHER OBJECT:

But elsewhere Jesus gave other disciples the same prerogatives as Peter; for example, the power to "bind and loose."[6] Peter might have had a good deal of authority, but he was not some kind of supreme leader of the apostles — or the whole Church — as Catholics wrongly think.

Nor is there biblical evidence about a supposed "papal succession." Why should the office and position of Peter — whatever it might have been — apply to anyone else?

THE ONE-MINUTE APOLOGIST SAYS:

Yes, it's true that Jesus gave graces and privileges to all the apostles; but that only underscores how significant it was that Peter alone received the "keys of the kingdom."

These "keys" clearly related to the office of stewardship, which was held by a single man, not a group. The other apostles along with Peter could impose ecclesiastical penalties ("bind") and give absolution for sins ("loose"), just as Catholics believe priests and bishops can do today. But this doesn't mean there can't be other powers reserved for the higher office of the papacy. And indeed, that Jesus apparently withheld the "keys" from the other apostles, while conspicuously granting them to Peter, suggests very strongly that He meant for Peter alone to possess the powers they signify.

As for Peter's office being perpetual (having successors), it is instructive to once again look at the analogy of the "steward" in the Old Testament monarchy. The Jewish kings had a succession of stewards serving them. When Jesus came He restored the throne of David — and also the office of chief steward. Peter was thus the chief bishop of the Church, and he lived and died in Rome. So his successors, the bishops of Rome, fill the office that Peter held: the papacy. That was the point of Jesus' parallel with the Old Testament stewards. This was understood by Jewish hearers at the time, but today we need to learn about the structure of Hebrew royal households.

It's also just plain logical. If there is biblical warrant for a leader of the Church, it stands to reason that this would be a perpetual office, just as all the other gifts and offices are ongoing. Why should there be a leader for only one or two generations?

✠

*"So Peter, in T.W. Manson's words, is to be 'God's viceregent. . . .
The authority of Peter is an authority to declare what is right
and wrong for the Christian community. His decisions
will be confirmed by God.'"*

THE NEW BIBLE DICTIONARY (PROTESTANT REFERENCE WORK)

[1]cf. Rev. 3:7, Job 12:14 [2]e.g., Gen. 43:19, 1 Kings 4:6, 18:3, 2 Kings 10:5, 18:18, 1 Chron. 27:33, Isa. 22:15 [3]R.T. France, in Morris, Leon, general editor, *Tyndale New Testament Commentaries* [4]F. F. Bruce, *The Hard Sayings of Jesus* [5]Oscar Cullmann, *Peter: Disciple, Apostle, Martyr* [6]Mt. 18:7-8, Jn. 20:23

Peter himself is not the "rock" to which Jesus referred

The Church cannot be built on the foundation of a sinful man. Rather, Jesus was talking about Peter's *faith* — the true Rock.

THE ONE-MINUTE APOLOGIST SAYS:
Because names were highly important in the biblical and Hebrew worldview,[1] Jesus' renaming of Simon as "Rock" provides much insight into the role our Lord had in mind for him.

Matthew 16:18 is a crucial text for understanding Peter's place among the Apostles, and the office of the papacy throughout the ages:

"And I tell you, you are Peter, and on this rock I will build my church, and the powers of death shall not prevail against it."

Following a straightforward reading of the passage, Catholics believe that "rock" refers to Peter himself (it is the meaning of "Peter" — Greek: *Petros* — after all). Many Protestants through the years have contended that "rock" referred instead to Peter's faith, not his person (perhaps Jesus even meant to contrast the two). In this way, they could avoid the pro-papacy implications of the Catholic view.

Today, the traditional Catholic interpretation is accepted by the majority of biblical scholarship, even if many rank-and-file Evangelicals still dispute it. The great Baptist exegete D.A. Carson, for example, wrote:

[I]f it were not for Protestant reactions against extremes of Roman Catholic interpretation, it is doubtful whether many would have taken "rock" to be anything or anyone other than Peter. . . . In this passage Jesus is the builder of the church and it would be a strange mixture of metaphors that also sees him within the same clauses as its foundation.[2]

The Methodist scholar William F. Albright (with co-author C.S. Mann) makes the following remarkable observation:

[O]ne must dismiss . . . any attempt to see this rock as meaning the faith, or the Messianic confession of Peter. . . . The general sense of the passage is indisputable . . . Peter is the rock on which the new community will be built, and in that community, Peter's authority to "bind" or "release" will be a carrying out of decisions made in heaven. His teaching and disciplinary activities will be similarly guided by the Spirit to carry out heaven's will.[3]

A PROTESTANT MIGHT FURTHER OBJECT:

The proper Greek word for "rock" was *petra*, meaning a "huge stone," whereas Peter's new name was different: *Petros*, meaning "little stone" or "pebble." So Jesus was not calling Peter a rock; He was *contrasting* him with a rock. He was reminding Peter that He alone was the foundation upon which the Church was built.

THE ONE-MINUTE APOLOGIST SAYS:

In the Koine Greek dialect of the New Testament, *petros* and *petra* are in fact synonyms. In an inflected language like Greek, the endings of words can signify gender, and in this case, Peter was called *Petros* because that was the masculine variation of the word. In the Aramaic language in which Matthew was originally written, the word *kepha* would have been used in both cases. This is why in the gospels we see Peter sometimes referred to as "Cephas" or "Kephas" — a carryover of the Aramaic into the Greek translation. As D.A. Carson points out: "Had Matthew wanted to say no more than that Peter was a stone in contrast with Jesus the Rock, the more common word would have been *lithos* ("stone" of almost any size). Then there would have been no pun — and that is just the point!"

Moreover, this interpretation makes no sense, because in this metaphor Jesus is the *builder* or architect of the Church, not its foundation. Peter is the foundation upon which He builds. This is not unprecedented. Scripture elsewhere describes men as being the "foundation" of the Church:

> **1 Peter 2:5**: "[L]ike living stones be yourselves built into a spiritual house, to be a holy priesthood."

> **Ephesians 2:19-22** "[T]the household of God, built upon the foundation of the apostles and prophets, Christ Jesus himself being the cornerstone, in whom the whole structure is joined together and grows into a holy temple in the Lord; in whom you also are built into it for a dwelling place of God in the Spirit."

Therefore, it is perfectly plausible for Peter to be described as the foundation of the Church (in a preeminent sense; thus showing his leadership), since priests, apostles, and prophets are also described in the same way (collectively).

✠

"[Petros] describes not so much Peter's character (he did not prove to be 'rock-like' in terms of stability or reliability), but his function, as the foundation-stone of Jesus' church. . . . The word-play, and the whole structure of the passage, demands that this verse is every bit as much Jesus' declaration about Peter as v.16 was Peter's declaration about Jesus."

R.T. FRANCE (ANGLICAN BIBLE COMMENTATOR)

[1]e.g., Gen. 17:5, 15, 32:28 [2]Frank E. Gaebelein, ed., *Expositor's Bible Commentary* [3]William F. Albright, *Anchor Bible*, vol. 26

Paul rebuked Peter

This shows that Peter wasn't infallible,
and that Paul had at least equal authority.

THE ONE-MINUTE APOLOGIST SAYS:
*Paul rebuked Peter for hypocrisy; however this has
no bearing on Peter's ecclesiastical or teaching authority.*

Many seem to be confused about the Catholic teaching on the papacy, wrongly think-
ing that if popes are protected from teaching error by the Holy Spirit, they must
therefore be perfect human beings, too (and Peter manifestly was not!). This objection stems from the following passage:

> **Galatians 2:9, 11-14**: "And when they perceived the grace that was
> given to me, James and Cephas [Peter] and John, who were reputed to
> be pillars, gave to me and Barnabas the right hand of fellowship. . . . But
> when Cephas came to Antioch I opposed him to his face, because he
> stood condemned. For before certain men came from James, he ate with
> the Gentiles; but when they came he drew back and separated himself,
> fearing the circumcision party. And with him the rest of the Jews acted
> insincerely, so that even Barnabas was carried away by their insincerity.
> But when I saw that they were not straightforward about the truth of
> the gospel, I said to Cephas before them all, 'If you, though a Jew, live
> like a Gentile and not like a Jew, how can you compel the Gentiles to
> live like Jews?'"

Hypocrisy and other human failings are nothing new. Peter had already denied Jesus
three times; Paul himself had persecuted Christians before his conversion; King David
committed adultery and murder; Moses murdered a man early in his life, and so forth.
God has only sinners to work with, yet work with them He does.

Since the present case deals with human failing, not authority, it really has nothing to
do with papal infallibility, which protects the pope only from definitively teaching error,
and only on matters of faith and morals. Neither does it suggest that Paul's authority was
equal to or greater than Peter's. In fact, quite the contrary: Peter's greater authority is
implied in Paul's reference to Peter's ability to "compel the Gentiles to live like Jews."

A PROTESTANT MIGHT FURTHER OBJECT:

If indeed Paul knew that Peter was the first "pope" and the leader of the Church, then he would have been way out of line rebuking Peter in public in this manner.

Paul accuses him of gross negligence and of not being "straightforward about the truth of the gospel." This seems to involve more than a mere rebuke for bad behavior. Therefore, he didn't know Peter was the "pope" because it wasn't true in the first place!

THE ONE-MINUTE APOLOGIST SAYS:

First of all, "speaking truth to power" is not an unknown biblical theme (for example, the prophet Nathan's rebuke of King David in 2 Samuel 12:1-15), nor is a rebuke of a pope inconceivable in Catholic thought and history. In fact, great saints such as St. Francis and St. Catherine of Siena have done precisely that, and it didn't contradict the Catholic doctrine of the papacy.

As for this particular situation, it is not even absolutely clear from what little information we have that Paul was totally right and Peter completely wrong. The prominent Protestant scholar James D.G. Dunn wrote about this question[1] and pointed out that since we have only Paul's report, we can't finally decide who was right and who was wrong. He thinks that the internal evidence of the passage provides clues suggesting that even Paul himself didn't think he was decisively correct, over against Peter: "If Paul had won, and if Peter had acknowledged the force of his argument, Paul would surely have noted this, just as he had strengthened his earlier position by noting the approval of the 'pillar apostles' in 2:7-10."

Dunn even goes so far as to assert that Paul was likely "defeated at Antioch, that the church as a whole at Antioch sided with Peter rather than with Paul," and points out that Paul seemed to "change his tune" afterward, in later epistles to the Romans and Corinthians falling in line more with the policies of Peter and Barnabas:

> [I]t can hardly go unnoticed that Paul's advice to such communities . . . is more in line with the policy of Peter and Barnabas at Antioch than in accord with his own strongly worded principle in Gal. 1:11-14!

St. Paul's own words and actions, then, pull the remaining teeth from this argument against the papacy.

✠

"[Galatians 2] gives us a glimpse of Peter at Antioch, the first church with a significant ex-pagan element, sharing table-fellowship with the Gentile converts, and then meeting a barrage of Jewish-Christian opposition, in the face of which he withdraws. This defection was roundly denounced by Paul; but there is no hint of any theological difference between them, and Paul's complaint is rather the incompatibility of Peter's practice with his theory. The old theory . . . of persistent rivalry between Paul and Peter, has little basis in the documents."

THE NEW BIBLE DICTIONARY (PROTESTANT REFERENCE WORK)

[1] *Unity and Diversity in the New Testament*

How can a mere man be infallible?

We know that all men make mistakes;
only God doesn't. Thus the doctrine of papal
infallibility places a mere man on the level of the divine.

THE ONE-MINUTE APOLOGIST SAYS:
*With God all things are possible. If He chooses to protect a man
from error, He can do so. In fact, we see this occurring in Scripture.*

Infallibility, according to the Catholic Church, means that the Pope (and the decisions of an ecumenical council in agreement with the Pope) cannot err in a teaching on faith or morals that is intended as binding on all Catholics.

Infallibility isn't the same thing as "inspiration" — Catholics don't believe that the Pope speaks with the voice of the Holy Spirit — and it doesn't guarantee that a pope will be morally perfect, or even especially intelligent or wise. Infallibility is a supernatural gift granted by God's grace alone, for His purposes, in order to uphold and make known (with certainty, in faith) His spiritual and theological truth.

Since infallibility is a lesser gift than inspiration, it should not surprise us any more than, or seem less plausible than, our belief (shared with Protestants) that God worked through the writers of the Bible to produce an infallible book. Why couldn't a God who worked through men to produce an infallible Bible continue to work through men to preserve the infallible teachings that flow from it, for all time? After all, some of the Bible's authors, such as David, Paul, and Matthew, had also been great sinners at one time.

Infallibility is likewise less extraordinary than the gift of prophecy. Prophets routinely purported to proclaim the very "word of the LORD," a kind of "revelation on the spot." This is a much greater claim than papal infallibility, which is primarily a preventive, or "negative" guarantee, not positive inspiration.

Even in Old Testament times, God granted certain men this gift of special protection from error, as it suited Him. For example, the Levites, who were teachers, among other things:

> **Malachi 2:6-8**: "True instruction was in his mouth, and no wrong was found on his lips. He walked with me in peace and uprightness, and he

turned many from iniquity. For the lips of a priest should guard knowledge, and men should seek instruction from his mouth, for he is the messenger of the LORD of hosts."

A Protestant Might Further Object:

Those graces were given a long time ago, each time for purposes specific to their time and place. Prophets had to have a special word from God to proclaim His message to Israel and to prepare for the coming of Jesus. The authors of Scripture were given a special one-time gift to produce the Bible so that Christians could have an infallible authority.

And so even if the apostles had some kind of charism of infallible teaching, it, too, was meant only for the time when the gospel was first proclaimed. There's no reason to think that any such gift exists today.

The One-Minute Apologist Says:

On the contrary, it makes perfect sense that God should continue to offer those gifts to His Church — unless we think the Church's mission over the last nineteen centuries is any less important to God than that of the prophets or Apostles.

The prophets received their inspiration by the Holy Spirit.[1] The Holy Spirit is now given to all Christians[2]: is it not reasonable that an even greater measure of the Holy Spirit would be given to leaders of the Church, who have the responsibility to teach? Jesus reassured His disciples — those first official teachers of the Church — "When the Spirit of truth comes, He will guide you into all the truth."[3]

Few faithful Evangelical Protestants would deny that God has the power to grant a gift like infallibility (or prophecy, or inspiration) to men. Those who make an argument like this either misunderstand the claim of infallibility, or are simply asserting in different words their contention that God *didn't* give that gift to Peter and his successors.

"If Christianity is both social and dogmatic, and intended for all ages, it must humanly speaking have an infallible expounder. Else you will secure unity of form at the loss of unity of doctrine, or unity of doctrine at the loss of unity of form; you will have to choose between a comprehension of opinions and a resolution into parties, between latitudinarian and sectarian error. You may be tolerant or intolerant of contrarieties of thought, but contrarieties you will have. By the Church of England a hollow uniformity is preferred to an infallible chair; and by the sects of England, an interminable division. Germany and Geneva began with persecution, and have ended in scepticism. The doctrine of infallibility is a less violent hypothesis than this sacrifice either of faith or of charity. It secures the object, while it gives definiteness and force to the matter of the Revelation."

John Henry Newman

[1]2 Chron. 24:20, Neh. 9:30, Zech. 7:12 [2]Jn. 15:26, 1 Cor. 3:16
[3]Jn. 16:13; cf. 8:32

The case of Pope Honorius proves that popes are not infallible

If this heretical pope could err so greatly when teaching doctrine, how can we believe that popes are infallible?

THE ONE-MINUTE APOLOGIST SAYS:

If Pope Honorius (r. 625-638) truly did hold the heresy of Monothelitism, he nonetheless did not teach it officially or make it a required belief for all Catholics; therefore, the doctrine of papal infallibility was not contradicted.

The First Vatican Council (1870) definitively explained how and when a papal proclamation is considered infallible (emphasis added):

> We teach and define that it is a dogma divinely revealed: that the Roman Pontiff, when he speaks *ex cathedra,* that is, when, in discharge of the office of pastor and teacher of all Christians, by virtue of his supreme Apostolic authority, he *defines a doctrine regarding faith or morals to be held by the universal Church,* is, by the divine assistance promised to him in Blessed Peter, possessed of that infallibility with which the divine Redeemer willed that His Church should be endowed.

Without getting into unnecessary and complicated details, it's enough to note that Pope Honorius's statements in support of Monothelitism (belief that Jesus had only one will rather than two — one divine and one human — wills) are to be found in private letters, not public, official teaching pronouncements. His condemnation as a heretic by the ecumenical Council of Constantinople in 681 does not prove or even imply otherwise. Honorius might have personally been a heretic (as some scholars believe), but no one believes that he ever used his office to teach his heresy or to make it binding on the entire Church.

And other scholars deny that his letters contained any heresy, or they contend that Honorius simply chose his words poorly. Still others think that Honorius was only condemning the notion that Christ had two *contrary* wills (or at least two not-entirely-harmonious wills), which is a correct and orthodox thing to do.

In any of these scenarios, however, papal infallibility, as understood by Catholics for centuries, is completely unharmed. The Honorius case, although widely considered the very best historical evidence against papal infallibility, is really just a huge red herring. Catholics freely acknowledge that popes can privately err in theological matters — as in any other area, like any other man. A pope who hasn't studied, prayed, and meditated on the mysteries of Christ won't enjoy any special knowledge or insights simply by virtue of the infallibility of his office. A pope who doesn't nurture the gift of faith in his heart won't, simply because the Holy Spirit protects him from teaching error in an official capacity, find it any easier to avoid doubt and yes, even heresy in his personal theological convictions. Once again we see fundamental misunderstanding of the doctrine of infallibility underlying Protestant arguments against it.

A PROTESTANT MIGHT FURTHER OBJECT:

All right, but Honorius wasn't the only notorious example of an erring pope.

How about Liberius and Vigilius? They taught heresy too. Don't their cases also illustrate the falsity of infallibility?

THE ONE-MINUTE APOLOGIST SAYS:

These two incidents do not disprove Catholic infallibility, either — not individually nor considered together. Again, the necessary conditions were simply not met.

Opinions differ as to whether Liberius (r. 352-366) caved in and signed an Arian statement. (Arianism was a rampant heresy in the early Church that denied the full divinity of Christ.) But if so, it was as a result of being imprisoned by the Arian emperor Constantine, under threats of possible execution or torture. That hardly qualifies as the free, willful promulgation of a doctrine.

It's true that Vigilius (r. 537-555) flip-flopped and wavered on some Christological questions, too, appearing to agree with certain heresies (Monophysitism and Nestorianism). But one letter where he supposedly accepted the former heresy is regarded by many scholars as a forgery. Emperor Justinian had seized the pope by force and imprisoned him, and it seems the weak Vigilius made questionable statements under coercion and duress, much as Liberius had.

In any event, the nature of the statements made by these popes, and the conditions under which they were made, do not fall under the sphere of infallibility. God gives the popes their charism of infallibility not for their personal enjoyment, but for them to be able to teach Christian truth to the whole Church, according to the promise of Jesus.[1] Only in such cases can it be said to operate; and not once in the long history of the Catholic Church has a pope taught moral or doctrinal error in such an instance.

✝

"Honorius's crime was not heresy itself, but his refusal to act against heresy when he should have by issuing an authoritative proclamation of the orthodox Catholic Faith.
"[W]hile we can certainly criticize Pope Honorius for his failure to act responsibly in his office, his behavior has nothing to do with papal infallibility. He was neither declaring dogma nor teaching officially. . . . Not careful enough, yes. Heretical, no."

PATRICK MADRID (CATHOLIC APOLOGIST)

[1] Jn. 14:25-26

The Priesthood

The Bible says we're *all* priests

All of us now share in Christ's universal priesthood. That means there is no special class of believer set apart from others in the Church.

THE ONE-MINUTE APOLOGIST SAYS:
The Bible teaches that there is such a thing as clergy,
who are set apart from lay members of the Church,
and it also gives indication of priestly function.

The priesthood as we know it today is not a strong motif in the New Testament. But this can be explained in terms of development of doctrine: in the early days of Christianity some things were understood only in a very basic or skeletal sense. This is true even of certain doctrines accepted by all Christians, such as the Holy Trinity or original sin. The canon of biblical books took four centuries to be fully established.

Also, it has been argued that priesthood was a subdued feature of primitive Christianity because it had not yet finally separated from Judaism; therefore, the authority of Jewish priests was still accepted. Acts 2:46 describes the Jerusalem Christians as "day by day, attending the Temple together and breaking bread in their homes." The Apostle Paul was presenting offerings in the Temple around the year 58,[1] acknowledged the authority of the Jewish high priest, described himself as a "Pharisee,"[2] and observed Jewish feasts.[3]

But one can indeed find evidence of a Christian priesthood in the Bible. At the Last Supper Jesus entrusts to His disciples a remembrance of the central aspect of the liturgy or Mass (consecration of the bread and wine).[4] Paul may also have presided over a Eucharist in Acts 20:11. These same disciples were models of a priestly life: wholly devoted to God, fulfilling a lifelong calling. Jesus had chosen and "appointed" them, and they had become His "friends."[5] He was their sole master.[6] There was no turning back in their ministry,[7] and they were called to a radical commitment involving even leaving possessions and their entire families.[8] The priest-disciple must accept hardships and privations and embrace self-denial,[9] and (if so called) celibacy, for the sake of undistracted devotion to the Lord.[10] They served the Body of Christ,[11] and dispensed sacraments.[12] A universal priesthood of "offering" (sacrifice) extending to "every place" in New Testament times is prophesied in Isaiah 66:18, 21 and Malachi 1:11.

Protestants sometimes cite 1 Peter 2:5, 9 (cf. Revelation 1:6, 5:10, 20:6) to the effect that all Christians are priests; therefore there is no set-apart priestly ministry. But Peter was citing Exodus 19:6: "You shall be to me a kingdom of priests and a holy nation." This passage couldn't possibly have meant that there was no priesthood among the ancient Hebrews, since in Leviticus they clearly had a separate class of priests. In fact, this same chapter twice contrasts the "priests" with the "people."[13] Thus, it makes much more sense to interpret "priests" in 1 Peter 2:5 as meaning a chosen, specially holy people. This is fairly clear in context, in both parallel passages. The notion of "spiritual sacrifices" (faith, praise, giving to others) applies to all Christians.[14]

A PROTESTANT MIGHT FURTHER OBJECT:

How can Catholics explain calling their priests "Father" in light of Matthew 23:9?

There Jesus told us plainly, "And call no man your father on earth, for you have one Father, who is in heaven."

THE ONE-MINUTE APOLOGIST SAYS:

Jesus spoke those words during the course of rebuking the Pharisees for spiritual pride. Here He was using the common Hebrew method of exaggeration or hyperbole[15] to teach that God the Father is the ultimate source of all authority. It's absurdly literal to think He meant to prohibit all uses of the word "father"; for what would we call the man married to our mother?

Nor are we to think Jesus was prohibiting use of the term "father" in a spiritual sense, for the New Testament authors use it this way in numerous places, e.g.:

Acts 7:2: "And Stephen said: 'Brethren and fathers, hear me. The God of glory appeared to our father Abraham.'"

1 Corinthians 4:15: "For though you have countless guides in Christ, you do not have many fathers. For I became your father in Christ Jesus through the gospel."

✠

"But they will be priests of God and of Christ, and will reign with him for a thousand years' [Rev. 20:6]. This clearly does not mean only the bishops and presbyters, who are now called by the distinctive name of 'priests' in the Church; but just as we call all Christians 'Christs' in virtue of their sacramental anointing (chrisma) so we call them all 'priests' because they are members of the one Priest. And the apostle Peter says of them that they are 'a holy people, a royal priesthood' [1 Pet. 2:9]."

ST. AUGUSTINE

[1]Acts 21:26 [2]23:5-6 [3]20:6 [4]Lk. 22:19 [5]Jn. 15:15-16 [6]Mt. 6:24 [7]Lk. 9:62 [8]Mt. 4:22, 19:27, Lk. 14:26 [9]Mt. 8:19-20, 10:38, etc. [10]Mt. 19:12, 1 Cor. 7:7-9 [11]1 Cor. 3:5, 9:19, 2 Cor. 4:5 [12]1 Cor. 4:1, Jas. 5:14, Mt. 28:19 [13]Ex. 19:21-24 (cf. Josh. 3:6, 4:9) [14]Phil. 2:17, Heb. 13:15-16 [15]See Mt. 19:24, 23:24, Lk. 6:42

Celibacy for priests is both unnatural and unbiblical

A man is meant to have one wife,
as most of the early Church leaders did.

THE ONE-MINUTE APOLOGIST SAYS:

*Quite the contrary, celibacy is expressly recommended by Jesus and the
Apostle Paul as a way to serve the Lord wholeheartedly with fewer distractions.*

Many Protestants object to the Catholic tradition of celibacy among priests, nuns, and monks. But one wonders why, since the Bible clearly teaches that this is a very good thing:

Matthew 19:12: "For there are eunuchs who have been so from birth, and there are eunuchs who have been made eunuchs by men, and there are eunuchs who have made themselves eunuchs for the sake of the kingdom of heaven. He who is able to receive this, let him receive it."

1 Corinthians 7:7-9: "I wish that all were as I myself am. But each has his own special gift from God, one of one kind and one of another. To the unmarried and the widows I say that it is well for them to remain single as I do. But if they cannot exercise self-control, they should marry. For it is better to marry than to be aflame with passion."

1 Corinthians 7:32-35, 38: "The unmarried man is anxious about the affairs of the Lord, how to please the Lord; but the married man is anxious about worldly affairs, how to please his wife, and his interests are divided. And the unmarried woman or girl is anxious about the affairs of the Lord, how to be holy in body and spirit; but the married woman is anxious about worldly affairs, how to please her husband. I say this for your own benefit, not to lay any restraint upon you, but to promote good order and to secure your undivided devotion to the Lord. . . . So that he who marries . . . does well; and he who refrains from marriage will do better."

The Western or Latin Rite of the Catholic Church (in its smaller Eastern rites, married priests are traditionally permitted) draws its priests from among those men who have felt called by God to give "undivided devotion to the Lord."[1] This cannot be "unnatural," because it is a gift and calling from God, and it is not anti-biblical, because it follows Paul's own instructions!

Every institution has the right to make whatever rules it deems necessary in order for it to fulfill its purpose. Most people are called to marriage; some few are called to be celibate. The Catholic Church doesn't hinder God or any individual in the least, but rather, cooperates with God's own will for each man.

A Protestant Might Further Object:

But the Bible also teaches that Peter was married,[2] as were other unspecified apostles.[3] And in 1 Timothy 3:2 Paul even casually mentions that bishops were, or could be, married. How can the Church today forbid what the Apostles permitted?

The One-Minute Apologist Says:

There is reason to believe that these married apostles renounced their married state, for precisely the reasons that Jesus and Paul pointed out.

As for 1 Corinthians 9:5, the disciples indeed had a right to get married, but they renounced it. Paul did exactly the same thing regarding remuneration for missionary work (which he writes about in the same chapter), for the sake of the gospel — "above and beyond the call of duty," so to speak. This is perfectly harmonious with the Catholic position. Jesus Himself taught that a person might even leave his wife (by mutual consent) and everything else, in order to be a profoundly committed disciple:

> **Luke 18:29-30:** "[T]here is no man who has left house or wife or brothers or parents or children, for the sake of the kingdom of God, who will not receive manifold more in this time, and in the age to come eternal life."

> **Matthew 19:27-29:** "Then Peter said in reply, 'Lo, we have left everything and followed You. What then shall we have?' Jesus said to them, '. . . every one who has left houses or brothers or sisters or father or mother or children or lands, for my name's sake, will receive a hundredfold, and inherit eternal life.'"

It's quite possible that St. Peter separated from his wife in this way; the Bible never mentions his wife traveling with Jesus and the disciples at all, even though it mentions many other women (several by name) who encouraged the disciples, and who helped support them financially.[4] Even those Eastern Catholic and Orthodox priests who are married regularly abstain from relations with their wives for long periods, for various liturgical or penitential reasons. The Bible clearly supports this practice, too.[5]

"By his law of celibacy the priest, so far from losing the gift and duties of fatherhood, rather increases them immeasurably, for, although he does not beget progeny for this passing life of earth, he begets children for that life which is heavenly and eternal."

Pope Pius XII (r. 1939-1958)

[1] 1 Cor. 7:35 [2] Mk. 1:30, Lk. 4:38 [3] 1 Cor. 9:5 [4] Mt. 27:55-56, Mk. 15:40-41, Lk. 8:1-3, 23:49, 55, 24:10, 22 [5] 1 Cor. 7:5

The Catholic Church's male-only priesthood is sexist

Men and women are equal in Christ,[1] so why can't a woman be a priest? Jesus certainly did not discriminate against people in this way.

THE ONE-MINUTE APOLOGIST SAYS:
The Church's all-male priesthood doesn't signify that women are inferior to men, only that they have different roles to play within the Body of Christ.

One reason for the male-only priesthood is very straightforward: Jesus Christ was a man. During Mass a priest stands in place of Christ (since it is, properly speaking, Christ Himself, not the priest, who offers the Sacrifice and performs the supernatural consecration), thus it is fitting that only men are ordained. Accordingly, none of the twelve disciples chosen by Jesus to be the first priests were women. And Scripture presupposes that only men were to be ordained and to serve as priests or elders or bishops.[2]

Neither Jesus nor the Church, in following Jesus, can rightly be accused of "sexism." Indeed, the person whom the Church venerates as the very highest, most exalted and sublime of God's created beings — Jesus' own mother, the Blessed Virgin Mary — is a woman; no man ever had the immense, unfathomable honor of "bearing God." It was a woman (Mary Magdalene) who had the privilege first to see the risen Jesus, and of course Jesus showed extraordinary regard for women throughout His public ministry.

By the same token, the Catholic Church reveres women in its official documents and teachings, and offers as role models many strong, brilliant women saints and biblical heroines from throughout the Church and salvation history. (No Church can be sexist that exalts such women as St. Catherine of Siena, St. Teresa of Avila, St. Thérèse of Lisieux, St. Edith Stein, and Mother Teresa.)

Perhaps "unisexists" object also to the fact that God chose to become incarnate in a male body? Maybe God should have come as a sexless eunuch or a woman? On what basis can mere fallen human beings (of either sex) question the will and wisdom of Almighty God? Many of this mindset justify their views by questioning Holy Scripture (either its content, or its faithful manuscript transmission). But very few scholars would deny that Jesus was a man. The Catholic Church can't call to the priesthood a woman who wasn't given a certain gift and vocation — by virtue of God's will — any more than it could call a man to bear a child and suckle it after birth.

A PROTESTANT MIGHT FURTHER OBJECT:

But it was patriarchal society, not God, that created these artificial, unnatural, unjust barriers between the sexes.

The different "roles" you speak of aren't found in Scripture; rather they were imposed by a patriarchal Church operating in a patriarchal society.

THE ONE-MINUTE APOLOGIST SAYS:

Jesus Himself laid the framework for gender roles within the Church. True, He did not specifically say, "Do not ordain women," yet He did not include women among His disciples, whom Catholics believe were the model for the priesthood. Was Jesus simply bound by "patriarchal" cultural conventions? Well, nowhere else does He give indication of being "anti-woman," and we know that he was never shy about over-turning conventions. Indeed, His whole life can be seen as a revolutionary subversion of the social order. So if it were His will that women should be priests, certainly that would have been made clear, and some of the disciples would have been women.

Also, if it were God's will for His Church to ordain women priests, then it surely would have happened, because Catholics believe in faith that the Holy Spirit guides the Church. Could a Church guided by the Holy Spirit commit this great injustice to half the human race for 2,000 years? Certainly God can overcome any obstacle, including men who wanted to "keep women down" or exclude them for improper reasons. But if someone believes that God is unable to work His purposes despite a "patriarchal culture," then the problem lies in lack of faith in God, or in falsely accusing God Himself.

The existence of roles of greater and lesser authority (of one sort at least), do not mean that those with one role are greater or lesser than others. If women are suppos-edly unequal to men in the Catholic Church (and Christianity, generally), then Jesus is also not equal to the Father, since He subjected Himself to the Father,[3] and even to Mary and Joseph.[4] The Holy Trinity itself provides an edifying analogy, showing us a clear example of an equality-of-being that nevertheless includes (by its very nature) subjection and differing roles.

✠

> *"All salvation depends on the decision which she [Mary] made*
> *in the words Ecce ancilla; she is united in nine months'*
> *inconceivable intimacy with the eternal Word; she stands*
> *at the foot of the cross. . . . Such is the record of Scripture.*
> *Nor can you daff it aside by saying that local and temporary*
> *conditions condemned women to silence and private life.*
> *There were female preachers. One man had four daughters*
> *who all 'prophesied,' i.e., preached. There were prophetesses*
> *even in Old Testament times. Prophetesses, not priestesses."*

C. S. LEWIS

---

[1]Gal. 3:28 [2]1 Cor. 9:5, 1 Tim. 2:12, 3:2, 12
[3]Phil. 2:5-8; cf. 1 Cor. 11:3, 15:28 [4]Lk. 2:51

The Sacraments

The thief on the cross proves that sacraments are unnecessary

Jesus said that the thief on the cross next to Him would be saved,[1] yet he could not possibly have been baptized.

THE ONE-MINUTE APOLOGIST SAYS:
*In situations where a person cannot be baptized,
but would like to be, there is such a thing as a "baptism
of desire," but in circumstances where there is no hindrance
to receiving the sacrament, baptism is necessary for salvation.*

The Luke passage is nonetheless utilized as a proof text for denying the necessity of baptism and in fact of all the sacraments:

> **Luke 23:39-43**: "One of the criminals who were hanged railed at Him, saying, 'Are You not the Christ? Save Yourself and us!' But the other rebuked him, saying, 'Do you not fear God, since you are under the same sentence of condemnation? And we indeed justly; for we are receiving the due reward of our deeds; but this man has done nothing wrong.' And he said, 'Jesus, remember me when You come into Your kingdom.' And He said to him, 'Truly, I say to you, today you will be with me in Paradise.'"

From this biblical information, some non-sacramental Protestants conclude that baptism, and sacraments in general, are unnecessary for salvation. The weakness of their argument is that it assumes that the demands of an extraordinary situation also apply to ordinary situations. But one cannot take an exception and make it the rule; in fact, the existence of exceptions validates application of the rule in ordinary circumstances.

The example of the thief on the cross represents one such extraordinary situation. He had the desire for salvation, and thus would have chosen baptism if he had been given the chance. It would be unwise to take his case and make it the rule, but his case nonetheless shows us that salvation is somehow obtainable in circumstances apart from ordinary, sacramental baptism.

Here the Catholic belief in "baptism by desire" comes into play. By this the Church means a desire for water baptism by one who has a love of God, in faith, and sincere repentance and sorrow for one's sins (what is called "perfect contrition"). Another biblical example would be the account in Acts 10 of Gentile believers at the house of Cornelius, a

Roman centurion whom Peter encountered. The Holy Spirit "fell on" all of these men even before they were baptized. Thus, they were clearly accepted by God and had the desire to be included in the Christian fold, which included baptism as the "initiation rite." In this case, they were able to be baptized, and were, by Peter's command. But if circumstances had prevented it (for example, if they had been immediately arrested and imprisoned by other Romans), then they still could have been saved by the "baptism of desire." *The Catechism of the Catholic Church* explains in greater detail in paragraphs 1257-1260.

A Protestant Might Further Object:

But how can we know when something is an "exception"?

The judgment of whether something is "ordinary" or "extraordinary" is always debatable. The simpler and more straightforward interpretation is to say that Luke included this passage to teach us that sacraments are not necessary for salvation.

The One-Minute Apologist Says:

All rules have difficulties or exceptions or "loopholes" associated with them. That is one reason why law — and interpretation of law — exists, because the application is not always so straightforward, and it's often complex.

It is the same in theology and biblical interpretation. One can determine that there are general rules or theological truths, and then the question becomes: "How is this knowledge applied to all particular circumstances?" In this instance, we have many biblical indications of the necessity of baptism for a Christian.[2] That is the "rule."

Christianity has throughout history generally held to the necessity of baptism (if not always regenerative baptism). Furthermore, baptism is explicitly tied in with salvation in several passages.[3] It is certainly as necessary for a Christian to be baptized, as it is to "receive Jesus into your heart" (a common Protestant notion, but one never found in the Bible in those terms). But the Catholic Church is sensible enough to allow for situations or "loopholes" where it is impossible, without negating the overwhelming rule, as seen in the New Testament.

⊹

"[A] man may, without Baptism of Water, receive the sacramental effect from Christ's Passion, insofar as he is conformed to Christ by suffering for Him. Hence it is written (Rev. 7:14): 'These are they who are come out of great tribulation, and have washed their robes and have made them white in the blood of the Lamb.' In like manner a man receives the effect of Baptism by the power of the Holy Ghost, not only without Baptism of Water, but also without Baptism of Blood: forasmuch as his heart is moved by the Holy Ghost to believe in and love God and to repent of his sins: wherefore this is also called Baptism of Repentance."

St. Thomas Aquinas (1225-1274)

[1]Lk. 23:39-43 [2]Mt. 28:19, Col. 2:11-12, John 4:1-2, Eph. 4:5, Acts 10:48, Gal. 3:27 [3]Acts 2:38, 1 Pet. 3:21; cf. Mk. 16:16, Rom. 6:3-4, John 3:5, Acts 22:16, 1 Cor. 6:11, Titus 3:5

Holy Communion was meant to be a symbolic rite only

According to the Bible, the Lord's Table is a memorial of Christ's death, not a miraculous re-creation of His Body.

THE ONE-MINUTE APOLOGIST SAYS:
Holy Scripture contains several passages that clearly prove Jesus and Paul taught a Real Presence of Jesus' Body and Blood in the Holy Eucharist.

In fact, it is difficult to imagine how the Real Presence could have been expressed any more strongly than it was. Jesus proclaimed at the Last Supper, "Take, eat; this is my body"[1] and "This is my blood of the covenant, which is poured out for many for the forgiveness of sins."[2] The same Blood (His own) that was shed for forgiveness was miraculously present in the cup at the Last Supper, according to Jesus. Luke records the same equation concerning the eucharistic bread: "This is my Body which is given for you."[3] In His discourse in John 6, Jesus is extremely explicit about His meaning:

> **John 6:53-58:** "So Jesus said to them, 'Truly, truly, I say to you, unless you eat the flesh of the Son of man and drink His blood, you have no life in you; he who eats my flesh and drinks my blood has eternal life, and I will raise him up at the last day. For my flesh is food indeed, and my blood is drink indeed. He who eats my flesh and drinks my blood abides in me, and I in him. As the living Father sent me, and I live because of the Father, so he who eats me will live because of me. This is the bread which came down from heaven, not such as the fathers ate and died; he who eats this bread will live for ever.'"[4]

St. Paul follows this realism by referring to the eucharistic "cup of blessing" as "participation in the Blood of Christ" and the consecrated bread as "participation in the Body of Christ."[5] He even goes so far as to say that anyone partaking of Holy Communion "in an unworthy manner" would be "guilty of profaning the Body and Blood of the Lord."[6] This is not the language of metaphor or symbolism; it is literal language. This is why the Church teaches "transubstantiation": that the bread and wine undergo a change of substance and become the true Body and Blood of Christ.

In rejecting this teaching, Protestants have simply departed (to varying degrees) from 1,500 years of an unbroken eucharistic tradition of realism. They argue, for example, that Jesus was talking symbolically in John 6, because of the metaphor of "bread." Yet, at the Last Supper, He equates the bread with His body; and Paul does the same thing in 1 Corinthians. If the Eucharist were meant to be simply a symbol, both Jesus and St. Paul could have made it clear. Instead, Jesus' true meaning was so plain that "many of his disciples" found it very difficult to accept and left Him.[7] Why did He not simply explain that He was speaking symbolically? Why did He not clear up such a gross misunderstanding?

Elsewhere in the gospels, when Jesus was misunderstood in His teachings, He carefully and fully explained His meaning so that even the most obtuse could grasp it.[8] But in this case He demanded "radical" faith, a gift that had to be "granted" by God the Father.[9] And when His hearers stubbornly refused to believe, Jesus habitually repeated the same "hard teaching"[10] rather than explain that He was simply misunderstood. This strongly implies that He knew they were being obstinate and refusing to believe, rather than that He was unclear in His wording.

A Protestant Might Further Object:

In the Bible, true miracles are always able to be verified by witnesses. Yet transubstantiation cannot be verified in this way. How do we know that this strange doctrine wasn't just made up by the Scholastic theologians of the Middle Ages who wrote about "the number of angels that could dance on the head of a pin," and so forth?

The One-Minute Apologist Says:

The miracle of the Virgin Birth cannot be "proven" by witness verification; neither can Jesus' redemptive sacrifice on the Cross. Likewise the Eucharist involves a different kind of miracle, requiring more faith. Jesus did indeed perform many "outward" miracles in order to verify His divinity, but He also called for a more sublime, trusting faith. The Pharisees once requested a sign of Him, but He answered them, "An evil and adulterous generation seeks for a sign; but no sign shall be given to it except the sign of the prophet Jonah."[11]

Jesus appealed to this "sign" of His Resurrection even as he disparaged the demand for signs. He taught that no signs or miracles would suffice for hard-hearted people[12] ("If they do not hear Moses and the prophets, neither will they be convinced if someone should rise from the dead"). Hence in John 20 when He appeared to His disciples — including "Doubting Thomas" — to prove He was raised from the dead, He told them solemnly, "Blessed are those who have not seen and yet believe."

✠

"How I hate this folly of not believing in the Eucharist! If the gospel be true, if Jesus Christ be God, what difficulty is there?"

Blaise Pascal

---

[1]Mt. 26:26; cf. Mk. 14:22, 1 Cor. 11:24 [2]Mt. 26:28; cf. Mk. 14:24, Lk. 22:20, 1 Cor. 11:25 [3]Lk. 22:19 [4]cf. Jn. 6:31-52, 59-71 [5]1 Cor. 10:16 [6]1 Cor. 11:27; cf. 11:29, 1 Cor. 10:16 [7]Jn. 6:60-64 [8]Mt. 16:5-12, 19:24-26, Jn. 3:1-15, 4:31-34, 8:21-34, 11:11-14 [9]Jn. 6:65 [10]Mt. 9:2-7, Jn. 8:56-58 [11]Mt. 12:38-39 [12]Lk. 16:31

The Catholic Mass is an abomination in the sight of God

Jesus doesn't die again and again on the altar. In the New Covenant, His death on the Cross once for all has made any ongoing sacrifice unnecessary.

THE ONE-MINUTE APOLOGIST SAYS:

Catholics don't believe that Jesus "dies again and again" at every Mass. Rather, His one sacrifice,[1] which transcends time, is re-presented.

Jesus' sacrifice is not only present to us on earth, but also in heaven, where the book of Revelation tells us there is an "altar"[2] at which Jesus and the prayers of the saints[3] are offered. In Revelation, Jesus is also called the "Lamb" twenty-eight times, clearly meant to hearken back to the Old Testament sacrificial system of priests' offering unblemished lambs to atone for sin.

Further, the Apostle Paul, in 1 Corinthians 10:14-22, uses the language of "tables," suggesting that he viewed the Eucharist as a sacrifice. He mentions the "altar" of the Old Covenant in 10:18 and makes a direct analogy to the New Covenant, over against the altars and sacrifices of the pagans:

> **1 Corinthians 10:19-21:** "What do I imply then? That food offered to idols is anything, or that an idol is anything? No, I imply that what pagans sacrifice they offer to demons and not to God. I do not want you to be partners with demons. You cannot drink the cup of the Lord and the cup of demons. You cannot partake of the table of the Lord and the table of demons."

Jesus is now our High Priest, having offered Himself as a sacrifice for our sins.[4] In the historical sense, this is a past event, but in the timelessness of God and heaven, it is an "eternally present" event.

> **Revelation 5:6:** "And between the throne and the four living creatures and among the elders, I saw a Lamb standing, as though it had been slain. . . ."

This is highly significant, because it describes as a present event in heaven the historical sacrifice of Jesus on Calvary in Jerusalem (precisely as Catholics believe occurs at Mass). This same "slain Lamb" (Jesus) is repeatedly described as sitting on God's throne,[5] and a "golden altar" is in front of this throne.[6] It appears, then, that such sacrificial,

"Catholic"-type worship is the status quo in heaven, because Jesus offers Himself, as a priest, "forever."[7] Heavenly worship is a worthy model for earthly Christian worship.

A PROTESTANT MIGHT FURTHER OBJECT:

The symbolic language of Revelation and the Jewish-directed specific language of Hebrews shouldn't be applied to Christian worship. If that were the intention, it would have been made much more clear by Paul in "teaching passages."

THE ONE-MINUTE APOLOGIST SAYS:

No Christian would deny that Jesus is the High Priest of the whole human race — not just of the Jews. That is not a "Jewish-directed" concept.

Scenes depicting sacrificial worship in Revelation cannot simply be dismissed. Their meaning is significant; even if they are not a narrative of literal events, they have a true meaning, as all Scripture does. And so we see clear support in the Bible for the Catholic conception of priestly, sacrificial worship. Paul uses the same categories and reveals a strong "eucharistic realism" in 1 Corinthians 10:14-22 and 11:23-30. Other passages present a similar picture of universal sacrifices, Eucharist, and "offering":

> **Genesis 14:18**: "And Mel-chiz'edek king of Salem brought out bread and wine; he was priest of God Most High."

> **Leviticus 23:13**: "And the cereal offering with it shall be two tenths of an ephah of fine flour mixed with oil, to be offered by fire to the LORD, a pleasing odor; and the drink offering with it shall be of wine, a fourth of a hin."

> **Isaiah 66:18, 21**: "For I know their works and their thoughts, and I am coming to gather all nations and tongues. . . . And some of them also I will take for priests and for Levites, says the LORD."

> **Malachi 1:11**: "For from the rising of the sun to its setting my name is great among the nations, and in every place incense is offered to my name, and a pure offering; for my name is great among the nations, says the LORD of hosts."

✢

> *"[T]he pagans have built temples for their gods, they have set up altars, established priesthoods and offered sacrifices, whereas we Christians construct, in honor of our martyrs, not temples, as if to gods, but memorial shrines, as to men who are dead, but whose spirits are living with God. We do not in those shrines raise altars on which to sacrifice to the martyrs, but to the one God. . . . They are not invoked by the priest who offers the sacrifice. For, of course, he is offering the sacrifice to God, not to the martyrs . . . because he is God's priest, not theirs. Indeed, the sacrifice itself is the Body of Christ."*

ST. AUGUSTINE

[1]Heb. 7:27 [2]Heb. 6:9, 8:3-5, 9:13, 11:1, 14:18, 16:7 [3]Heb. 5:8-9, 8:3-4
[4]Heb. 3:1, 4:14-16, 5:10, 6:20, 7:23-26, 8:1 [5]Rev. 7:17, 22:1, 3 [6]Rev. 8:3
[7]Ps. 110:4, Heb. 6:20, 7:17, 24

The Catholic Mass
is a form of idolatry

No less so than the golden calf, or the
idolatry of Jeroboam. The ancient pagans
worshiped statues, and Catholics worship bread.

THE ONE-MINUTE APOLOGIST SAYS:
Catholics worship the Lord Jesus Christ, whom
they believe is truly present in the Holy Eucharist.

Some non-Catholic Christians claim that Catholics are guilty of worshiping false gods
— that is, of idolatry — in the Mass, but this is an utterly groundless charge. It comes
about because some forms of Protestantism (especially the Calvinist tradition) are
unbiblically iconoclastic (i.e., opposed to use of any images in worship). Yet Jesus
Himself held up bread in His hands and said, "This is my body" and told His disciples to do the same in memory of Him (which would make Him an idolater, too,
since He suggested an image).

Granted, the Eucharist is interpreted differently by various Christians, but how does
belief in the real, substantial presence of Jesus in the Eucharist somehow move
Catholics into the realm of outright idolatry and "Baal-worship"? The Bible gives a
clear-cut example of what this looks like, in the narrative describing the idolatry of
Jeroboam:

> **1 Kings 12:28, 32**: "So the king took counsel, and made two calves of
> gold. And he said to the people, 'You have gone up to Jerusalem long
> enough. Behold your gods, O Israel, who brought you up out of the land
> of Egypt' . . . and he offered sacrifices upon the altar; so he did in Bethel,
> sacrificing to the calves that he had made."

> **1 Kings 14:9**: "[Y]ou have done evil above all that were before you and
> have gone and made for yourself other gods, and molten images, provok-
> ing me to anger, and have cast me behind your back."

Jeroboam did not intend to worship Yahweh (the true God) through the use of these
graven images, but rather, "other gods": a rank expression of polytheism. We know that
he offered sacrifice to these molten images, making this a case of true idolatry and a
direct violation of the Commandments. Other instances of idolatry also involved

images representing other gods, not the one true God.[1] But in the Catholic Mass, the object of worship is the one God Himself.

A Protestant Might Further Object:

But Exodus 32 (Aaron and the Golden Calf) disproves the Catholic position.

The Jews were attempting to worship Yahweh through images, just like Catholics do, and God condemned this through Moses.

The One-Minute Apologist Says:

We know this is untrue from the text itself, for Aaron recounted that the people had told him, "Make us gods."[2]

Obviously, they could not have had Yahweh in mind at that point, since they knew that He is not "made by hands" and is eternal. Then they said that these gods would "go before us." The most straightforward interpretation of that is the golden calf being carried before them. Certainly they could not have thought (even in their debased state of mind) that Yahweh Himself could be compelled to do such a thing. Therefore, they must have regarded the calf as a pure idol of their own making, not as a mere representation of the true God. The people exclaimed, "These are your gods, O Israel, who brought you up out of the land of Egypt!" Nowhere were the Jews permitted to build a calf as an "image" of God. This was an outright violation of the injunctions against "molten images."[3]

Multiple "gods" fall under the absolute prohibition of polytheism that was known to any observant Hebrew.[4] Lastly, Psalm 106:19, 21 states that they "exchanged the glory of God for the image of an ox" and "forgot God." How, then, can it be said that they were consciously worshiping the true God and not an idol? Thus, the attempted comparison to the Real Presence in the Eucharist completely fails.

Idolatry involves states of mind. The devout, orthodox Catholic is certainly not angry, distrustful, or "forgetting" God during the consecration, but rather, worshiping Him and giving Him all the glory, and "remembering" Him, too, just as Jesus explicitly commanded. This is a separate issue from whether or not a supernatural change occurs. And a Protestant may, in fairness, acknowledge that.

⊹

"It may be asked whether there was any difference in principle between the use of bull-calf images to support Yahweh's invisible presence and the use of cherubs for the same purpose in the holy of holies at Jerusalem. The answer probably is that the cherubs were symbolical beings (representing originally the storm-winds) and their images were therefore not 'any likeness of anything that is in heaven above, or that is in the earth beneath, or that is in the water under the earth,' whereas the bull-calf images were all too closely associated with Canaanite fertility ritual."

F. F. Bruce (Protestant Bible scholar)

[1] e.g., Ex. 32:1-5, 23, Ps. 106:19-21 [2] Ex. 32:23 [3] Ex. 34:17, Lev. 19:4, Num. 33:52, Deut. 27:15 [4] e.g., Ps. 106:19-23; cf. Hab. 2:18

It is wrong for Catholics not to allow everyone to receive Holy Communion

The Lord's Table should be open to all. What gives the Catholic Church the right to be so arrogant and exclusive?

THE ONE-MINUTE APOLOGIST SAYS:
The Holy Eucharist cannot be open to all because the Bible states that there is a doctrinal unity necessary before one receives communion. Catholics are simply following the biblical model.

Despite our differences, Catholics recognize as fellow Christians all validly baptized believers in Christ and the Holy Trinity. But receiving Holy Eucharist is among other things a symbol of complete unity: a supernatural communion of belief and practice. For Catholics to offer that symbol of unity to those who are not part of that communion would be dishonest and untrue to what they believe.

It's not a matter of arrogance, of "looking down" on anyone else, but rather, respect for the Eucharist and all that it means. Christian fellowship, unity in Jesus Christ in love, is supremely important, but so also is the doctrinal agreement that must accompany it, according to Paul's statement: "one Lord, one faith, one baptism."[1] Paul uses "faith" as a description of one body of truth, as in the following verses:

Acts 6:7: "[A] great many of the priests were obedient to the faith."

1 Timothy 1:2: "To Timothy, my true child in the faith."

1 Timothy 3:9: "[T]hey must hold the mystery of the faith with a clear conscience."[2]

1 Timothy 4:1, 6: "[S]ome will depart from the faith . . . nourished on the words of the faith and of the good doctrine which you have followed."[3]

Ephesians 4:5, understood with the above cross-references, offers a clear connection of at least one of the sacraments (baptism) with acceptance of a common set of doctrines: itself (i.e., one faith or tradition) something taught repeatedly by Paul elsewhere.[4]

A PROTESTANT MIGHT FURTHER OBJECT:
But this doesn't prove a direct relationship between doctrinal unity and the Eucharist. Most Christians agree on the central importance of baptism, but not on the nature and frequency of reception of Holy Communion.

Therefore, it is unreasonable for Catholics to exclude other Christians from the Lord's Supper, since the Christian Church as a whole continues to have these significant differences of opinion. When there are large differences, there should be more tolerance and understanding of those who differ.

THE ONE-MINUTE APOLOGIST SAYS:

From a Christian, biblical perspective, "what ought to be" is more important than "what is." Christians in fact disagree on the Eucharist, but it doesn't follow that they should do so, or that they are not required to achieve unity in this matter, as in all others.

Those who hold firm to what they believe is true, traditional doctrine will always be accused by some of being "intolerant," no matter what. In 1 Corinthians 10:16 and 11:27-30, Paul clearly shows that he regards the Eucharist as the literal Body and Blood of Christ. Therefore, the Real Presence is part of the apostolic deposit of faith which Paul passed down and urged people to accept in faith, in its entirety.

Moreover, in the same context, we also see his concern for doctrinal unity in the Body of Christ:

> **1 Corinthians 11:17-19:** "But in the following instructions I do not commend you, because when you come together it is not for the better but for the worse. For, in the first place, when you assemble as a church, I hear that there are divisions among you; and I partly believe it, for there must be factions among you in order that those who are genuine among you may be recognized."[5]

Right after his strong statement of the Real Presence, Paul stresses unity:

> **1 Corinthians 10:16-17:** "The cup of blessing which we bless, is it not a participation in the Blood of Christ? The bread which we break, is it not a participation in the Body of Christ? Because there is one bread, we who are many are one body, for we all partake of the one bread."

It is all of a piece: doctrinal unity, unity in love, and the Eucharist. The Catholic view, then, is eminently biblical: there is one faith, and the Eucharist, as a symbol and sign of this doctrinal unity, is the actual Body and Blood. That is the received faith, according to Paul. If someone disbelieves this, he shouldn't partake of the Eucharist.

✠

"This is not some terrible oppressive tradition of men that Catholics came up with in order to make outsiders feel miserable and inferior. Virtually every Christian communion holds to a creed or confession which is specifically intended to outline what that community believes; by definition, it must exclude those who disagree in some sense (possibly including Holy Communion among other things). This is simply obedience to the tradition passed down from the Apostles."

ST. IGNATIUS OF ANTIOCH (D.C. 110)

---

[1]Eph. 4:5 [2]cf. Jude 3, Gal. 1:23, Titus 1:4, 2 Tim. 1:13-14, 2:2 [3]cf. Jn. 17:23
[4]e.g., Rom. 16:17, 1 Cor. 1:10, Phil. 1:27, 2:2, 2 Thess. 2:15, 3:6 [5]cf. 11:2

Baptism is merely a symbolic rite

Nothing supernatural occurs;
water is just a picture or parable of being saved.

THE ONE-MINUTE APOLOGIST SAYS:
The Bible teaches that baptism confers spiritual regeneration,
washes away sins, and initiates a person into the Christian faith.

The Bible often teaches that baptism is far more than a mere symbol. In fact, few things are expressed more clearly in Holy Scripture. Peter states outright: "Repent, and be baptized every one of you in the name of Jesus Christ for the forgiveness of your sins,"[1] and: "Baptism . . . now saves you."[2] Likewise, the apostle Paul recounts what he had been told to do after his conversion to Christianity, and how it was interpreted: "Rise and be baptized, and wash away your sins, calling on His name";[3] and writes in Titus 3:5: "He saved us . . . by the washing of regeneration." Paul makes a strong statement on baptismal regeneration in the midst of his extended treatise on justification:

> **Romans 6:3-4:** "Do you not know that all of us who have been baptized into Christ Jesus were baptized into His death? We were buried therefore with Him by baptism into death, so that as Christ was raised from the dead by the glory of the Father, we too might walk in newness of life."

Furthermore, in Romans 6:3-4 and Colossians 2:11-13, St. Paul regards forgiveness as one of the results of baptism. According to his frequent analogy of baptism to the Resurrection of Christ,[4] he teaches that we were spiritually dead — as Jesus was physically dead[5] — before we "were buried with Him in baptism."[6] After baptism (parallel to the Resurrection itself), we have new life and forgiveness of original sin[7] and the indwelling of the Holy Spirit.[8]

Lastly, there is the evidence of Mark 16:16. Some Bible scholars question that this chapter is authentic (it doesn't appear in some early manuscripts), but even if it's not, it still preserves the belief of early Christians — namely, that "He who believes and is baptized will be saved."

A PROTESTANT MIGHT FURTHER OBJECT:
But in John 3:3, 5, we learn that "water" is just a symbol. It doesn't actually "cleanse" anybody of sin. Rather, it is a metaphor for the Holy Spirit coming into a person's life.

Jesus was talking about born-again salvation, not baptism. Just as "born anew" is meant spiritually, not literally, so too are we to understand the water of baptism.

THE ONE-MINUTE APOLOGIST SAYS:

Let's look at this passage and compare it with some other related ones, according to the principle of "Scripture interprets Scripture":

> **John 3:3, 5**: "Jesus answered him, 'Truly, truly, I say to you, unless one is born anew, he cannot see the kingdom of God. . . . [U]nless one is born of water and the Spirit, he cannot enter the kingdom of God.'"

> **Titus 3:5**: "[H]e saved us, not because of deeds done by us in righteousness, but in virtue of His own mercy, by the washing of regeneration and renewal in the Holy Spirit."

> **1 Corinthians 6:11**: "But you were washed, you were sanctified, you were justified in the name of the Lord Jesus Christ and in the Spirit of our God."

Note the striking three-way parallelism:

> John: "enter the kingdom of God." / Titus: "He saved us" / 1 Corinthians: "you were justified."

> John: "born of water" / Titus: "washing of regeneration" / 1 Corinthians: "you were washed."

> John: "born of water and the Spirit" / Titus: "renewal in the Holy Spirit" / 1 Corinthians: "in the Spirit of our God."

The three passages taken together prove that baptism saves, justifies, regenerates, initiates us into the kingdom, and is related to the coming of the Holy Spirit. As we see in 1 Corinthians 6:11, God justifies and sanctifies: the *only* thing the believer does is get "washed" in baptism. Neither this passage nor its context contain anything about belief, or repentance, or the so-called "sinner's prayer."

The same applies to John 3:5 and Titus 3:5. In both passages God saves us or lets us enter the kingdom by His Holy Spirit. The only thing that we do is get baptized. This doesn't prove that nothing else is required, or that one can never lose the salvation thus gained, but it does show that baptism cannot be separated from salvation and justification, and that it has a saving power and grace, by God's will.

✠

"[W]hen sin and conscience oppress us . . . you may say: It is a fact that I am baptized, but, being baptized, I have the promise that I shall be saved and obtain eternal life for both soul and body . . . no greater jewel can adorn our body or soul than baptism; for through it perfect holiness and salvation become accessible to us, which are otherwise beyond the reach of man's life and energy."

MARTIN LUTHER

[1]Acts 2:38 [2]1 Pet. 3:21 [3]Acts 22:16 [4]cf. Rom. 8:11, 1 Cor. 15:20-23 [5]1 Cor. 15:22, Col. 2:13 [6]Col. 2:12; cf. Rom. 6:3-4 [7]Rom. 6:4, Col. 2:13 [8]Rom. 8:11

Infants cannot be baptized because they're not able to choose Jesus

The Bible teaches that people must
have first repented before receiving baptism.
First we must come to believe, then we can be baptized.

THE ONE-MINUTE APOLOGIST SAYS:

*The Bible contains many indications of infant baptism, which is why the
vast majority of Christians throughout history have believed and practiced it.*

The Bible contains no explicit command to baptize infants. But then, neither does it
expressly prohibit it; nor does it tell us only to baptize adult believers, or those old
enough to have made a free decision to believe in Jesus. What we can know and learn
from the Bible on this matter is based on indirect indications. Even so, a fairly strong
case can be made for infant baptism. Acts 16:15 and 16:33 and 1 Corinthians 1:16
state that entire households or families were baptized:

Acts 16:15: "[S]he was baptized, with her household."[1]

Acts 16:33: "[H]e was baptized at once, with all his family."

1 Corinthians 1:16: "I did baptize also the household of Stephanas."

The question then comes down to, "What is a 'household'?" Was it likely to contain
children, some of them below the age of reason? In the biblical worldview (as in a com-
monsense view), "household" certainly strongly implied the inclusion of children. One
can find many examples of this:

Genesis 18:19: "[H]is children and his household after him."[2]

Genesis 36:6: "Then Esau took his wives, his sons, his daughters, and all
the members of his household."[3]

Genesis 47:12: "And Joseph provided his father, his brothers, and all his
father's household with food."[4]

Matthew 19:29: "And every one who has left houses or brothers or sisters
or father or mother or children or lands, for my name's sake."

Moreover, the Bible also refers to households becoming Christian believers, or
"saved" (e.g., Acts 11:14: "by which you will be saved, you and all your household"),

and teaches that infants are just as much a part of the covenant or Christian community as adults; e.g., Deuteronomy 29:10-12: "[Y]our little ones . . . may enter into the sworn covenant of the LORD."[5] This indicates that salvation is regarded as a communal as well as an individual thing. This is underscored by the apostle Paul's elaborate argument comparing baptism to circumcision.[6] Since circumcision was performed on eight-days-old boys, it stands to reason that he assumed baptism would also be performed on very young infants, or else why would he make such a comparison?

All of the above evidence suggests that infant baptism was thought to be a routine or normative practice.

A PROTESTANT MIGHT FURTHER OBJECT:

But Acts 2:38 connects baptism directly to repentance. This must rule out infant baptism, since infants are too young to repent.

THE ONE-MINUTE APOLOGIST SAYS:

The context of Acts 2:38 is the Day of Pentecost. A miracle had just occurred. The disciples were filled with the Holy Spirit and began speaking in tongues. A crowd had gathered to see what was happening, and those from many nations each heard tongues in their own language. In 2:14 Peter then stands up to "explain" to them what all the commotion was about. He interprets Pentecost and presents the gospel. At the end of his talk, the people are "cut to the heart" and they ask Peter and the apostles, "Brethren, what shall we do?"[7] Finally, in the verse in question, Peter replies, "Repent, and be baptized, every one of you, in the name of Jesus Christ for the forgiveness of your sins; and you shall receive the gift of the Holy Spirit."

This is a narrative account of an actual event, and Peter's answer is directed to those adults who asked him the question. It is clearly not meant to be a general prescription concerning the practice of baptism in the Church. Of course an adult must repent before baptism (as the Church teaches). This is what adult converts do; how they are accepted into the fold. But infants are not to be denied baptism's regenerative effects simply because they are incapable of repentance (and for that matter, are innocent of actual sin anyway).

✠

"We do the same in infant baptism. We bring the child with the conviction and trust that it believes, and pray God to grant it faith. But we do not baptize the child upon that; we do it solely upon God's command. Why so? Because we all know that God does not lie. I and my neighbor, in fact, all men, may err and deceive, but the Word of God cannot err."

MARTIN LUTHER

[1]cf. 10:24-48 with 11:14 [2]cf. 31:41 [3]cf. 1 Chron. 10:6 [4]cf. Num. 18:11 [5]cf. Gen. 17:7, Mt. 19:14 [6]Col. 2:11-13; cf. Rom. 4:11, 9:4, Gal. 3:14, 29 [7]Acts 2:37

The Catholic Church teaches that a baby who dies unbaptized will go to hell

How can it defend such a heartless belief?
Innocent babies have done nothing to earn damnation.

THE ONE-MINUTE APOLOGIST SAYS:
The Church doesn't have to defend this heartless belief because it doesn't hold it in the first place.

The Church nowhere teaches officially that babies who die without being baptized are automatically damned. In fact, the Church expressly denies it, for example, in the *Catechism of the Catholic Church*:

> 1261: "As regards children who have died without Baptism, the Church can only entrust them to the mercy of God, as she does in her funeral rites for them. Indeed, the great mercy of God who desires that all men should be saved, and Jesus' tenderness toward children which caused Him to say: 'Let the children come to me, do not hinder them,'[1] allow us to hope that there is a way of salvation for children who have died without Baptism. All the more urgent is the Church's call not to prevent little children coming to Christ through the gift of holy Baptism."

Such teaching is closely related to the larger concept of baptism of desire, which the Church has long held, as noted in the *Catechism*:

> 1257: "God has bound salvation to the sacrament of Baptism, but He Himself is not bound by His sacraments."

> 1258: "The Church has always held the firm conviction that those who suffer death for the sake of the faith without having received Baptism are baptized by their death for and with Christ. This Baptism of blood, like the desire for Baptism, brings about the fruits of Baptism without being a sacrament."

This "baptism of blood" has also been applied to intentionally aborted children.

> 1259: "For catechumens who die before their Baptism, their explicit desire to receive it, together with repentance for their sins, and charity, assures them the salvation that they were not able to receive through the sacrament."[2]

The previous considerations and passages apply to babies who die before being baptized, insofar as they, too, are unable to receive the sacrament and too young to desire it. The *Catechism* (1281) muses, "It may be supposed that such persons would have desired Baptism explicitly if they had known its necessity." In this Catholics trust in God's merciful nature. But in any event, the Church doesn't teach (like some strains of Protestant Calvinism) that all these babies go to hell.

A PROTESTANT MIGHT FURTHER OBJECT:

This position as you explain it seems too ambiguous.

If indeed, Catholics don't think all unbaptized babies who die go to hell, then why doesn't the Church adopt the position that babies receive understanding when they reach the afterlife and are then allowed to choose? Or that all of them are automatically saved?

THE ONE-MINUTE APOLOGIST SAYS:

Catholics deny that one can have a second chance at salvation after death (souls in purgatory are already saved; they just have to be cleaned up a bit to enter heaven). That can be established from Scripture, for example, Hebrews 9:27: "just as it is appointed for men to die once, and after that comes judgment"). And "automatic salvation" goes beyond what we can know from the Bible.

If the Catholic position is a bit ambiguous, that's because we simply can't know all the answers to this question. That's why some Catholics have believed in limbo, a place where the unbaptized saved live forever in a state of natural happiness. Limbo (literally, "border") is a very old and widely held concept, but is not dogmatically binding (it's not even mentioned in the *Catechism*). Many theologians throughout history (such as the Greek Fathers and St. Thomas Aquinas) thought of limbo as a condition of natural happiness. Its inhabitants do not enjoy the Beatific Vision (beholding God face-to-face) as the blessed in heaven do. But it is nonetheless far more like heaven than hell.

The truly severe difficulties in this regard belong to the school of "supralapsarian" Calvinists, who hold that God absolutely predestined the damnation of certain human beings from eternity: even before the fall of man. This would include infants, who obviously couldn't do anything whatsoever to avoid reprobation if they had been predestined for hell. The Catholic Church denies that this is true of any unsaved person, let alone infants. Limbo, as one commonly suggested solution to this difficult scenario, preserves both God's infinite mercy and justice, as pertains to original sin.

"It is believed that infants in limbo know and love God intensely by the use of their natural powers, and they enjoy full natural happiness."

FR. JOHN A. HARDON, S.J.

[1]Mk. 10:14; cf. 1 Tim. 2:4 [2]cf. 1260, 1281

Confession to a priest
is an unbiblical concept

Why can't we just go to God for forgiveness?
He doesn't need an intermediary to show us His mercy.

THE ONE-MINUTE APOLOGIST SAYS:
The Bible teaches in many passages that
there exists a special class of clergy who have the
authority to hear confessions and the power to forgive sins.

Those who deny as unbiblical the forgiveness of sins by God through priests must somehow account for the many biblical passages indicating confession to another human being of higher spiritual authority. For example: "They were baptized by him [John the Baptist] in the river Jordan, confessing their sins";[1] "Many also of those who were now believers came [to St. Paul], confessing and divulging their practices."[2]

The disciples (models for the later priesthood), had the power to "bind and loose": rabbinic terms for responsibilities which included hearing confession and dispensing forgiveness as God's representative ("loosing"), or, on the other hand, handing out penances ("binding").

Matthew 18:18: "Truly, I say to you, whatever you bind on earth shall be bound in heaven, and whatever you loose on earth shall be loosed in heaven."

John 20:23: "If you forgive the sins of any, they are forgiven; if you retain the sins of any, they are retained."

2 Corinthians 2:10: "Any one whom you forgive, I also forgive. What I have forgiven, if I have forgiven anything, has been for your sake in the presence of Christ."

In its article on "Forgiveness," *The International Standard Bible Encyclopedia*, a Protestant work, explains that the power of "binding and loosing" "clearly implies the possession of the power to forgive sins."

Often people will say, "Why can't we just go straight to God to confess?" In many instances, according to Catholic teaching, we can. We are ordinarily required to confess to a priest only in cases of grave, mortal sin (though it is highly encouraged for lesser sins). But the first reason we also go to the priest is because this is biblical teaching, as seen in the passages above.

It is also quite reasonable. God often includes men in His processes and plans. He uses us to help proclaim His Good News. He also wants us to pray for each other, so that He can give more grace and blessings to others. And in light of human nature, confessing to another human being is both more indicative of sincere repentance and more psychologically satisfying than confessing to the unseen God.

A Protestant Might Further Object:

But the Bible also clearly tells us to confess to one another.[3] So why do Catholics think we must confess only to a priest?

The One-Minute Apologist Says:

Making non-sacramental "confessions" of wrongdoing to one another, something that ought to happen where there is close friendship, humility, and mutual accountability of believers in Christ, does not at all rule out sacramental confession to a priest.

This is a false dilemma, a non-issue. The passages cited earlier describe something performed by priests in an official capacity: a special power reserved to them to forgive sins as a representative of God. James 5:16 ("confess your sins to one another") may refer to the former kind of confession, the kind connected with Christian fellowship.

Or perhaps it, too, refers to confession to a priest, since the preceding two verses specifically refer to calling "elders of the church" who pray for the sick, leading to a fruitful faith and forgiven sins. This would follow the example of confession being associated with important figures such as John the Baptist and Paul, above[4]), and with the authority of the Church.[5]

And the second part of this same verse reads: "The prayer of a righteous man has great power in its effects." Thus, the Bible says that we can go to a particularly holy or righteous person and receive more effect from his prayers. This is similar in concept to going to a righteous person (a priest, set apart to serve God and His Church), to receive more effect from the sacramental absolution and forgiveness of sins that he can grant us. So this passage — more closely examined — actually provides no disproof of Catholic confession at all.

The disciples were clearly a special class. Catholics believe they were the models for the priesthood (men specially called to serve God, as they were). Therefore, it is highly significant that they were granted this power to bind and loose and to forgive the sins of others not committed against them.[6] All of this is different from "confessing to one another," and is reasonably explained in the Catholic view.

✢

"The Catholic religion does not compel indiscriminate confession of sins;
it allows us to remain hidden from the sight of all other men, save one to whom
she bids us reveal the depths of our heart, and show ourselves as we are. . . .
Can anything be imagined more charitable, more tender?"

Blaise Pascal

[1]Mt. 3:6; cf. Mk. 1:5 [2]Acts 19:18 [3]Jas. 5:16 [4]Mt. 3:6,
2 Cor. 2:10 [5]Mt. 18:15-17 [6]Mt. 18:18, Jn. 20:21-23

Salvation

Works play no part whatsoever in salvation

God's grace saves us, not our good works.
That's why Paul taught the doctrine of "faith alone"[1]

THE ONE-MINUTE APOLOGIST SAYS:
Catholics agree that we are not saved by works. Yet the Bible teaches that
the true faith by which we are saved is accompanied and validated by works.

Romans 3:28 simply teaches that men are saved by faith (and God's grace), not works,
something that the Church has always affirmed in all its official teaching. Nowhere
does the Bible teach that we are saved by faith alone (the phrase never appears).
Ephesians 2:8-9 is often cited in support of "faith alone," but always without the very
important verse that follows: "For we are his workmanship, created in Christ Jesus for
good works, which God prepared beforehand, that we should walk in them."

Thus, in the entire three-verse passage, grace, faith, and works are all mentioned
together: indispensable for Christian salvation. This dynamic relationship is repeatedly
taught in the Bible, especially by the apostle Paul:

Romans 2:13: "For it is not the hearers of the law who are righteous
before God, but the doers of the law who will be justified."[2]

1 Corinthians 3:8-9: "Each shall receive his wages according to his labor.
For we are God's fellow workers; you are God's field, God's building."[3]

Galatians 5:6: "[F]aith working through love."[4]

Philippians 2:12-13: "[W]ork out your own salvation with fear and trem-
bling; for God is at work in you, both to will and to work for His good
pleasure."[5]

1 Thessalonians 1:3: "[Y]our work of faith and labor of love."[6]

James 1:22: "But be doers of the word, and not hearers only, deceiving
yourselves."[7]

James 2:14, 17: "What does it profit, my brethren, if a man says he has
faith, but has not works? Can his faith save him? . . . So faith by itself, if
it has no works, is dead."

James 2:22-26: "You see that faith was active along with his works, and faith was completed by works. . . . You see that a man is justified by works and not by faith alone. . . . For as the body apart from the spirit is dead, so faith apart from works is dead."

We see then that justification (being saved) and sanctification (being holy) are connected with one another. We are not saved apart from holy works, nor do our holy works save us independently of faith in Christ and His grace. Rather the two support and validate each other.

A Protestant Might Further Object:

But the Bible teaches that works are done out of gratefulness to God.

Good works are signs that we're already saved by grace through faith. A man who is justified will naturally show it by his good works.

The One-Minute Apologist Says:

If it is true that works have nothing whatsoever to do with salvation, then it is quite strange that in virtually every passage (including Paul's own) dealing with judgment and God's determination of whether a person is saved or lost, works are mentioned as key determinants, but faith is not.[8]

Matthew 7:19: "Every tree that does not bear good fruit is cut down and thrown into the fire."

Matthew 25:46: "And they [those who failed to do good works] will go away into eternal punishment, but the righteous into eternal life."

Of course Christians should perform good works out of gratitude to God. Every good thing a Christian does flows (or should flow) from his love for God and appreciation of the way of salvation that He makes possible through Jesus' sacrificial death on the Cross, and love for others. But this is not at all opposed to the Catholic view of the relationship of faith and works. We agree that works come from God's enabling grace alone, not our own self-generated natural powers, but we disagree that this somehow proves an already-attained salvation, based on many biblical texts clearly suggesting that salvation is a process[9] and can be lost.[10]

⁛

*"Christians have often disputed as to whether what leads
the Christian home is good actions, or Faith in Christ. . . .
It does seem to me like asking which blade in
a pair of scissors is most necessary."*

C. S. Lewis

[1]Rom. 3:28, Eph. 2:8-9 [2]cf. Heb. 5:9 [3]cf. 15:10, 58, Titus 1:15-16 [4]cf. 6:7-9 [5]cf. Titus 3:8, Heb. 6:9-10, 10:24 [6]cf. 2 Thess. 1:11 [7]cf. 1:23-27 [8]See also Mt. 5:20, 16:27, 25:31, 41-46, Lk. 14:13-14, Rom. 2:5-12, Heb. 5:9, 1 Pet. 1:17, Rev. 20:11-15, 22:12 [9]Phil. 2:12-13, 2 Pet. 1:10 [10]1 Cor. 9:27, 10:12, Gal. 5:4, Phil. 3:11-14, 1 Tim. 4:1, Heb. 3:12-14, 6:4-6, 2 Pet. 2:20-21

The Catholic system of "merit" is no different from works-salvation

The Catholic Church may say it doesn't teach salvation by works. But Catholics still believe that our "meritorious" good works help save us, rather than the free gift of grace.

THE ONE-MINUTE APOLOGIST SAYS:
Many non-Catholics only dimly understand the Catholic notion of merit. Rightly understood, it is indeed harmonious with salvation by "grace alone."

In the Catholic view, our meritorious actions do indeed contribute to our salvation. But they do not do so independently of God's freely given grace; in fact, to be effica-cious they must be entirely caused, preceded by, and "soaked in" God's grace. No good work is possible unless God acts in us first. Merit is God "crowning his own gifts," as the great Church father St. Augustine put it. This is not works-salvation, but grace responding to grace.

The Bible often indicates a reward for our actions (done only in God's grace). This is what Catholics mean by "merit" (emphases added):

Matthew 5:11-12: "Blessed are you when men revile you and persecute you and utter all kinds of evil against you falsely on my account. Rejoice and be glad, for your *reward* is great in heaven, for so men persecuted the prophets who were before you."[1]

Matthew 19:29: "And every one who has left houses or brothers or sisters or father or mother or children or lands, for my name's sake, will *receive a hundredfold*, and inherit eternal life."[2]

Luke 6:38: "Give, and it will be given to you; good measure, pressed down, shaken together, running over, will be put into your lap. *For the measure you give will be the measure you get back.*"[3]

1 Corinthians 3:6-9: "I planted, Apol'los watered, but God gave the growth. So neither he who plants nor he who waters is anything, but only God who gives the growth. He who plants and he who waters are equal, and each shall *receive his wages according to his labor.* For we are God's fel-low workers; you are God's field, God's building."[4]

Hebrews 10:35: "Therefore do not throw away your confidence, which has a great reward."[5]

Hebrews 11:6: "And without faith it is impossible to please Him. For whoever would draw near to God must believe that He exists and that He rewards those who seek Him."[6]

A Protestant Might Further Object:

But Catholics often speak in terms of having to "earn" heaven.

Does this not imply a system of rewards and punishments based on what man does, rather than what *God* does in freely offering us the grace of salvation won by Jesus Christ on the Cross?

The One-Minute Apologist Says:

Don't draw conclusions based on the mere use of words like "earn" and "merit." These are understood in the larger context of Catholic teaching on the universal necessity of God's grace for every good action on the part of man.

This is a classic case of confusion stemming from equivocal terminology. These words are always meant to signify our cooperation with God, not our own "goodness." They refer not to man's "earning" heaven as if by right, according to some standard of justice, but by gift, according to the rewards God has promised us — rewards infinitely greater than our token actions deserve.

Many Protestants deride the idea that we could "cooperate" with God at all; yet the Bible clearly teaches that we must do so (by His grace) in order to attain final salvation (see 1 Corinthians 3:9 above; also Mark 16:20: "And they went forth and preached everywhere, while the Lord worked with them"). In another verse, St. Paul expresses the thought perfectly:

2 Corinthians 6:1: "Working together with him, then, we entreat you not to accept the grace of God in vain."

If the Holy Spirit inspires, prompts, initiates our good works, leading to merit, how then can it be said that they "originate" with us? Catholics contend that human beings, enabled by grace, can cooperate with God: an explicit, undeniable, biblical, Pauline doctrine. God begins the process, and then we also participate in it.

✠

"With regard to the condition of salvation, it may be remembered that I allow, not only faith, but likewise holiness or universal obedience, to be the ordinary condition of final salvation."

"God works in you — therefore you must work. You must work together with Him, or He will cease working."

John Wesley (founder of Methodism)

[1]cf. Mk. 9:41, Jas. 1:12, Rev. 2:10, 3:11-12 [2]cf. 19:21 [3]cf. Col. 3:23-24
[4]cf. 3:14, 2 Cor. 9:6, 2 Tim. 4:8 [5]cf. 6:10, Matt. 20:4, 2 John
[6]cf. 1 Cor. 9:24-27; see also the *Catechism* 2008-2011

True Christian believers cannot fall away from salvation

We can identify God's "elect," and we
know they have absolute assurance of heaven.

THE ONE-MINUTE APOLOGIST SAYS:
Of course God gives eternal life to His elect. But we cannot be
absolutely sure who is among the elect, because we don't know the future
with certainty. For the Bible says that some people do fall away from faith.

The easiest and best way to dispel this false notion is first to cite the clear teachings
of the Bible (particularly from St. Paul):

1 Corinthians 9:27: "[B]ut I pommel my body and subdue it, lest after
preaching to others I myself should be disqualified."[1]

Galatians 5:1, 4: "[S]tand fast therefore, and do not submit again to a
yoke of slavery. . . . You are severed from Christ, you who would be justified by the law; you have fallen away from grace."[2]

Philippians 3:11-14: "[T]hat if possible I may attain the resurrection
from the dead. Not that I have already obtained this or am already
perfect; but I press on to make it my own, because Christ Jesus has
made me His own. Brethren, I do not consider that I have made it my
own. . . . I press on toward the goal for the prize of the upward call of
God in Christ Jesus."

1 Timothy 4:1: "Now the Spirit expressly says that in later times some
will depart from the faith by giving heed to deceitful spirits and doctrines of demons."[3]

Hebrews 3:12-14: "Take care, brethren, lest there be in any of you an
evil, unbelieving heart, leading you to fall away from the living God.
But exhort one another every day . . . that none of you may be hard-
ened by the deceitfulness of sin. For we share in Christ, if only we hold
our first confidence firm to the end."

Hebrews 6:4-6: "For it is impossible to restore again to repentance those
who have once been enlightened, who have tasted the heavenly gift, and

have become partakers of the Holy Spirit, and have tasted the goodness of the word of God, and the powers of the age to come, if they then commit apostasy."[4]

2 Peter 2:15, 20-21: "Forsaking the right way they have gone astray; they have followed the way of Balaam. . . . For if, after they have escaped the defilements of the world through the knowledge of our Lord and Saviour Jesus Christ, they are again entangled in them and overpowered, the last state has become worse for them than the first. For it would have been better for them never to have known the way of righteousness than after knowing it to turn back from the holy commandment delivered to them."[5]

A Protestant Might Further Object:

But if someone falls away, he obviously was never saved in the first place.

We can know with certainty that we are saved, based on 1 John 5:13 (cf. John 5:24): "I write this to you who believe in the name of the Son of God, that you may know that you have eternal life."

The One-Minute Apologist Says:

If such a person thought he was saved and a member of the elect, but actually was not (as later proved by his behavior), then he did not, in fact, "know" with absolute assurance that he was saved. Are we to say that all such people were pretenders, insincere phony Christians?

Much of 1 John is written in proverbial language. For example, verse 5:18: "We know that any one born of God does not sin."[6]

But of course, Christians sin all the time! (If sinning even once means that we were never a true Christian in the first place, there would be very few true Christians in the world.) Proverbial literature doesn't provide literal statements with no exceptions, but rather, common sense or general observations on certain states or conditions. In this case St. John is trying to express that a person in Christ should be righteous, and that sin is contrary to life in Christ.

In fact at first glance it appears that 1 John 5:18 is contradicted in 1 John 1:8: "If we say we have no sin, we deceive ourselves, and the truth is not in us." But we know that it is not a contradiction at all, because idealistic proverbial literature is not meant to be interpreted literally.

✠

"We are not bidden to distinguish between reprobate and elect —
that is for God alone, not for us, to do."

"He alone knows who are His."

John Calvin

[1]cf. 10:12 [2]cf. 10:12 [3]cf. 5:15 [4]cf. 10:23, 26, 29, 36, 39, 12:15
[5]cf. Rev. 2:4-5 [6]cf. 3:6, 8-9

Justification is external and imputed, not internal or "infused"

We don't actually become righteous; God only declares us so, because of the death of Jesus on the Cross.

THE ONE-MINUTE APOLOGIST SAYS:
This is not the teaching of the Bible, and it is a radical change from the doctrine that has been believed in the Church from the earliest times.

Catholics believe that justification and sanctification are connected, but Protestants think they're separate, that holiness has nothing directly to do with salvation; instead, God declares the sinner "righteous" and he instantly saved (justified) on the basis of the shed blood of Christ. The justified person will then perform good works in consequence of his justification.

However, the Bible teaches that sanctification is part and parcel of a process of salvation. It's not an optional "add-on" to salvation; it is central to it. Here are some biblical indications of an actual cleansing and removal of sins, rather than a declaration that sins are "covered over":

Acts 15:9: "[A]nd he made no distinction between us and them, but cleansed their hearts by faith."

Acts 26:18: "[T]o open their eyes, that they may turn from darkness to light and from the power of Satan to God, that they may receive forgiveness of sins and a place among those who are sanctified by faith in me."

1 Corinthians 1:2: "To the church of God which is at Corinth, to those sanctified in Christ Jesus."

1 Corinthians 6:11: "[Y]ou were washed, you were sanctified, you were justified in the name of the Lord Jesus Christ and in the Spirit of our God."

1 Peter 1:2: "[C]hosen and destined by God the Father and sanctified by the Spirit for obedience to Jesus Christ and for sprinkling with his blood."

2 Peter 1:9: "For whoever lacks these things is blind and shortsighted and has forgotten that he was cleansed from his old sins."

Note that in 1 Corinthians 6:11, justification and sanctification are placed together, both in the past tense. Sanctification is also a past event — part of justification — in the other epistolary verses cited above. It is the foundation for progress in the spiritual life, as St. Paul suggests in his farewell to the elders of the church in Ephesus:

> **Acts 20:32**: "And now I commend you to God and to the word of His grace, which is able to build you up and to give you the inheritance among all those who are sanctified."

A Protestant Might Further Object:

But what about Romans 5:19: "By one man's obedience, many will be made righteous." Doesn't that clearly teach imputed or forensic, declared justification? It speaks of people being made righteous, simply on account of Christ.

The One-Minute Apologist Says:

In that same verse, Paul speaks of the Fall, by which "many were made sinners." Yet original sin's effects on humanity were real and internal, and Paul draws an analogy between its effects and righteousness.

Thus it makes no sense to regard the sin as actual, but the righteousness as merely declared. Also, in verse 17, Paul connects "the abundance of grace" and "the free gift of righteousness," suggesting again that sanctification is directly related to justification, not separated from it.

The words and analogies that we find used throughout the Bible strongly suggest this "transformational" justification, not simply a declaration or imputation of righteousness. In 1 Chronicles 21:8, for example God is asked to "take away the iniquity of thy servant." King David, in his famous Psalm of profound repentance, does not separate sanctification from justification:

> **Psalm 51:1-2, 6-7, 9-10**: "Have mercy on me, O God, according to Thy steadfast love; according to Thy abundant mercy blot out my transgressions. Wash me thoroughly from my iniquity, and cleanse me from my sin! . . . Behold, Thou desirest truth in the inward being; therefore teach me wisdom in my secret heart. Purge me with hyssop, and I shall be clean; wash me, and I shall be whiter than snow. . . . Create in me a clean heart, O God, and put a new and right spirit within me."

St. Paul and the author of Hebrews teach the same organic closeness of justification and holiness, righteousness, or sanctification. We "share in a heavenly call"[1] — that is, to "be holy and blameless before Him."[2]

✝

"In like manner, Christ in us is said to be the hope of glory.
Christ then is our righteousness by dwelling in us by the Spirit: He justifies us
by entering into us, He continues to justify us by remaining in us. This is really
and truly our justification, not faith, not holiness, not (much less) a mere
imputation; but through God's mercy, the very presence of Christ."

John Henry Newman

[1]Heb. 3:1 [2]Eph. 1:41

There is no difference between "mortal" and "venial" sins

Sin is simply sin. Whoever commits even one sin is guilty of breaking all of the Law.[1]

THE ONE-MINUTE APOLOGIST SAYS:
The Bible plainly teaches that there is such a thing as a mortal sin and often refers to lesser and greater sins.

Some non-Catholic Christians think that all sins are exactly alike in the eyes of God: everything from a white lie to mass murder. They believe this not out of common sense, but because they erroneously think that the Bible teaches it.

Yet the Bible itself definitively refutes this notion:

1 John 5:16-17: "If any one sees his brother committing what is not a mortal sin, he will ask, and God will give him life for those whose sin is not mortal. There is sin which is mortal; I do not say that one is to pray for that. All wrongdoing is sin, but there is a sin which is not mortal."

Building on this biblical foundation Catholic theology identifies three conditions for commission of serious or "mortal" sin, whereby one ceases to be in a state of grace and is in danger of hellfire: 1) the act itself must involve very grave matter, 2) the sinner has to have sufficiently reflected on or had adequate knowledge of the sin, and 3) he must have fully consented by his will.

Scripture provides many indications of this difference in seriousness of sin, and of subjective guiltiness for it:

Luke 12:47-48: "And that servant who knew his master's will, but did not make ready or act according to his will, shall receive a severe beating. But he who did not know, and did what deserved a beating, shall receive a light beating. Every one to whom much is given, of him will much be required; and of him to whom men commit much they will demand the more."[2]

John 19:11: "[H]e who delivered me to you has the greater sin."

Acts 17:30: "The times of ignorance God overlooked, but now He commands all men everywhere to repent."[3]

1 Timothy 1:13: "[T]hough I formerly blasphemed and persecuted and insulted Him; but I received mercy because I had acted ignorantly in unbelief."

Hebrews 10:26: "For if we sin deliberately after receiving the knowledge of the truth, there no longer remains a sacrifice for sins."

The Bible often refers to sins that very well may exclude one from heaven. In Matthew 5:21-22 Jesus warns, "Whoever says, 'You fool!' shall be liable to the hell of fire." 1 Corinthians 6:9-10 tells us that "neither the immoral, nor idolaters, nor adulterers, nor sexual perverts, nor thieves, nor the greedy, nor drunkards, nor revilers, nor robbers will inherit the kingdom of God."[4] In like fashion, we read in Ephesians 5:5: "No fornicator or impure man, or one who is covetous (that is, an idolater), has any inheritance in the kingdom of Christ and of God." And James 1:15 says plainly that "desire, when it has conceived, gives birth to sin; and sin, when it is full-grown, brings forth death."

A PROTESTANT MIGHT FURTHER OBJECT:

But what about James 2:10? "For whoever keeps the whole law but fails in one point has become guilty of all of it."

Doesn't that prove that all sins are the same; that is to say, equally destructive and worthy of judgment?

THE ONE-MINUTE APOLOGIST SAYS:

This passage deals with man's inability to keep the Old Testament Law of God: a common theme in Scripture. It doesn't refer to moral commandments — as if to say that to commit even one small sin is to be guilty of every great sin.

In fact, James shows that he accepts differences in degrees of sin and righteousness elsewhere in the same letter: "[W]e who teach shall be judged with a greater strictness."[5] In 1:12, the man who endures trial will receive a "crown of life." James also teaches that the "prayer of a righteous man has great power in its effects";[6] this implies that there are relatively more righteous people, whom God honors by making their prayers more effective (for example, the prophet Elijah).

If there is a lesser and greater righteousness, then there are lesser and greater sins also, because to be less righteous is to be more sinful, and vice versa.

✠

"I would force upon men's notice that there are sins which do forfeit grace; and then if, as is objected, that we cannot draw the line between one kind of sin and another, this very circumstance will make us shrink not only from transgressions, but also from infirmities. From hatred and abhorrence of large sins, we shall, please God, go on to hate and abhor the small."

JOHN HENRY NEWMAN

[1]Jas. 2:10 [2]cf. Lev. 5:17, Lk. 23:34 [3]cf. Rom. 3:25
[4]cf. Gal. 5:19-21, Rev. 22:15 [5]3:1 [6]5:16

Original sin is not taught in the Bible

How can a baby be guilty of sin? God punishes people based on the actual sins they commit during their life.

THE ONE-MINUTE APOLOGIST SAYS:
Following Scripture's teaching, Christianity has always believed in the Fall of man. The entire human race rebelled against God and is corporately subject to sin, even from birth.

Catholics hold that the main effect of the Fall, of original sin, is concupiscence: which means a tendency to sin. (Protestant founders John Calvin and Martin Luther, on the other hand, taught a more profound fall, in which all men have a "sin nature.") Death itself is a consequence of the Fall; since no human is physically immortal, we are all therefore fallen.

The primary biblical passage in this regard is Romans 5:12, 15-18, where St. Paul asserts the reality of original sin in many ways:

"Therefore as sin came into the world through one man and death through sin, and so death spread to all men because all men sinned."

"[M]any died through one man's trespass."

"[J]udgment following one trespass brought condemnation."

"Because of one man's trespass, death reigned through that one man."

"[O]ne man's trespass led to condemnation for all men."

Many other passages also teach the notion of original sin:

Genesis 2:17: "[B]ut of the tree of the knowledge of good and evil you shall not eat, for in the day that you eat of it you shall die."

Genesis 3:9-11: "But the LORD God called to the man, and said to him, 'Where are you?' And he said, 'I heard the sound of Thee in the garden, and I was afraid, because I was naked; and I hid myself.' He said, 'Who told you that you were naked? Have you eaten of the tree of which I commanded you not to eat?'"

Psalm 51:5: "Behold, I was brought forth in iniquity, and in sin did my mother conceive me."

1 Corinthians 15:21-22: "For as by a man came death, by a man has come also the resurrection of the dead. For as in Adam all die, so also in Christ shall all be made alive."[1]

A Protestant Might Further Object:

But the Bible teaches that punishment was because of *actual* sin.

Romans 5:12 says, "Death spread to all men because all men sinned." Thus we "participate" in Adam's sin by choosing to do wrong as he did, not because we have inherited "original sin" from him.

The One-Minute Apologist Says:

Romans 5:12 needs to be interpreted in its context.

That context shows that we all were made subject to Adam's sin and its effects. For example, in the subsequent seven verses we read that "death reigned from Adam to Moses, even over those whose sins were not like the transgression of Adam," "many died through one man's trespass," "one man's trespass led to condemnation for all men," and "by one man's disobedience many were made sinners." 1 Corinthians 15:22, too, states that "in Adam all die" — not "because Adam's sin leads us to actual sin" or some such idea. Psalm 51:5, too, seems crystal-clear that sin is present in all of us even from the moment of conception. This "sin-nature" is not a result of anything we do — certainly not in the womb! — but is "inherited" by the children of Adam.

We have to be saved from this abnormal state. Most Christians throughout history have believed in infant and regenerative baptism, precisely because of the effects of original sin, and the need to counter them. The dominion of the Devil is a result of original sin, which caused a catastrophic cosmic disorder. That's why theological liberals who deny original sin invariably also deny the existence of the Devil and sometimes sin or evil as well.

⊹

"How could physical science find any traces of a moral fall? What traces did the writer expect to find? Did he expect to find a fossil Eve with a fossil apple inside her? Did he suppose that the ages would have spared for him a complete skeleton of Adam attached to a slightly-faded fig-leaf?"

"I am honestly bewildered as to the meaning of such passages as this, in which the advanced person writes that because geologists know nothing about the Fall, therefore any doctrine of depravity is untrue. Because science has not found something which obviously it could not find, therefore something entirely different — the psychological sense of evil — is untrue . . . it is all wild and whirling; as if a man said — 'The plumber can find nothing wrong with our piano; so I suppose my wife does love me.'"

G.K. Chesterton

[1]cf. 15:42-56

Eternal hellfire is not taught in the Bible

This is a myth made up to terrify people into becoming Christians. How could the loving God that Jesus preached doom people to everlasting torment?

THE ONE-MINUTE APOLOGIST SAYS:
The Bible contains many passages that undeniably teach the existence of eternal hellfire. Jesus actually talked more about hell than about heaven.

The essence of hell is separation from God, who says in effect: "So you want to live apart from me? Very well, then, go ahead." The Bible teaches that if men rebel, and ultimately refuse to repent, God gives them up to the hardening of their hearts.

This is not incompatible with God's love for us, but a necessary part of it. For God wants us to love Him freely, and He respects our freedom so much that He is willing to let men ultimately reject Him and spend eternity away from Him, if that is their choice. Christians want to proclaim the gospel so people can avoid that miserable fate, and can live eternally in God's wonderful presence forever.

The Bible contains many explicit passages on hell. Perhaps the most compelling one is Matthew 25:46, "[T]hey will go away into eternal punishment, but the righteous into eternal life." The same Greek word *(aionios)* is used for both "life" and "punishment." It's also used to describe unending punishment in the following passages:

Matthew 18:8: "[T]hrown into the eternal fire."

Matthew 25:41: "Then he will say to those at his left hand, 'Depart from me, you cursed, into the eternal fire prepared for the Devil and his angels.'"

Mark 3:29: "[B]ut whoever blasphemes against the Holy Spirit never has forgiveness, but is guilty of an eternal sin."

2 Thessalonians 1:9: "They shall suffer the punishment of eternal destruction and exclusion from the presence of the Lord and from the glory of His might."

Jude 7: "[J]ust as Sodom and Gomor'rah and the surrounding cities, which likewise acted immorally and indulged in unnatural lust, serve as an example by undergoing a punishment of eternal fire."

The related Greek word *aion* is used throughout Revelation for eternity in heaven,[1] and also for eternal punishment.[2] Some attempt to argue that Revelation 20:10 only applies to the devil, but they must explain Revelation 20:15: "[A]nd if any one's name was not found written in the book of life, he was thrown into the lake of fire." The "book of life" clearly has reference to human beings.[3]

A PROTESTANT MIGHT FURTHER OBJECT:

But how to explain Matthew 10:28? "And do not fear those who kill the body but cannot kill the soul; rather fear Him who can destroy both soul and body in hell." That doesn't sound like eternal torment, but rather, total annihilation. How can we exist in hell if our bodies and our souls are "destroyed"?

THE ONE-MINUTE APOLOGIST SAYS:

The word for "kill" here is the Greek *apollumi*, which means "ruin" or "lose," not extinction or literal destruction (cessation of existence). Other verses in which it appears[4] make this meaning clear. The same argument applies to Matthew 10:39, John 3:16, and 2 Peter 3:6-9. In the latter passage, for example, it is stated that the earth "perished" in Noah's flood. Obviously the earth was not annihilated, but wasted, consistent with the other interpretations above. Similarly, in Philippians 1:28, 3:19, and Hebrews 10:39, the words "destruction" and "destroyed" are from the Greek *apolia*. Its meaning as "ruin" is clearly seen in Matthew 26:8 and Mark 14:4 (a waste of ointment). In Revelation 17:8, when it refers to the Beast, it doesn't state that the Beast is wiped out of existence; but rather "it was and is not and is to ascend."

Other proof texts used by those who deny hell include Romans 1:32 and 6:21-2, and 1 John 5:16-17; but these either refer to physical or spiritual death, neither of which means "annihilation." The first is separation of body from soul; the second, separation of the soul from God. In 2 Peter 2:12, "destroyed" is the Greek word *kataphthiro*, but in the only other passage where it appears,[5] it is rendered "corrupt." If that verse were intended to teach annihilation, it would absurdly read, "men of nonexistent mind."

It should be added that we can't determine for sure from the Bible whether the "fire" of hell is literal, physical fire, or a typically pungent Hebrew metaphor for pain and suffering. Much of the popular conception of hell — clown-like caricatures of demons with pointed tails and pitchforks, and so forth — has no biblical basis. In any event, hell is a horrific place, and we all ought to do our utmost to avoid it.

✛

"Though our Lord often speaks of Hell as a sentence inflicted by a tribunal, He also says elsewhere that the judgment consists in the very fact that men prefer darkness to light, and that not He, but His 'word,' judges men. We are therefore at liberty . . . to think of this bad man's perdition not as a sentence imposed on him but as the mere fact of being what he is. The characteristic of lost souls is 'their rejection of everything that is not simply themselves.'"

C. S. LEWIS

[1]e.g., 1:18, 4:9-10, 5:13-14, 7:12, 10:6, 11:15, 15:7, 22:5 [2]14:11, 20:10 [3]cf. Rev. 3:5, 13:8, 17:8, 20:11-14, 21:27 [4]Mt. 10:6, Lk. 15:6, 9, 24, Jn. 18:9 [5]2 Tim. 3:8

The Church teaches that all non-Catholics will go to hell

But Jesus said, "If any one thirst, let him come to me and drink." So *anyone* who believes in Jesus can be saved.

THE ONE-MINUTE APOLOGIST SAYS:
The Catholic Church has never held that only its official members can be saved. But we believe that all are saved through the Church in some fashion, whether they are aware of it or not.

What do Catholics mean by "no salvation outside the Church"? This issue is a bit complicated and confusing, and so it needs to be carefully explained. Catholics believe that the Church is central to God's plan of salvation (1 Timothy 3:15: "the household of God, which is the church of the living God, the pillar and bulwark of the truth"), the earthly instrument through which, by the Holy Spirit, saving grace flows. Thus it benefits a man's prospects for salvation to be part of that Church, in order to partake of those saving graces most fully.

But not everyone is Catholic, and not every non-Catholic is personally culpable for not being one. For this there are many reasons: ignorance, bad personal experiences, a formation in erroneous teachings, not enough time or opportunity to be received, life-long adherence to other seemingly correct Christian traditions, and so forth. Something along these lines is indicated in biblical passages such as Romans 2:11-16:

> For God shows no partiality. All who have sinned without the law will also perish without the law, and all who have sinned under the law will be judged by the law. For it is not the hearers of the law who are right-eous before God, but the doers of the law who will be justified. When Gentiles who have not the law do by nature what the law requires, they are a law to themselves, even though they do not have the law. They show that what the law requires is written on their hearts, while their conscience also bears witness and their conflicting thoughts accuse or perhaps excuse them on that day when, according to my gospel, God judges the secrets of men by Christ Jesus.

Catholics do believe it's possible, then, not to be an official member of the Church and still go to heaven. The great medieval theologian St. Thomas Aquinas explains the Church's teaching in such cases:

If, however, some were saved without receiving any revelation, they were not saved without faith in a Mediator, for, though they did not believe in Him explicitly, they did, nevertheless, have implicit faith through believing in Divine providence, since they believed that God would deliver mankind in whatever way was pleasing to Him.

With regard, however, to Cornelius,[1] it is to be observed that he was not an unbeliever, else his works would not have been acceptable to God, whom none can please without faith. Now he had implicit faith, as the truth of the Gospel was not yet made manifest: hence Peter was sent to him to give him fuller instruction in the faith.

A PROTESTANT MIGHT FURTHER OBJECT:

But what about Pope Boniface VIII and his famous letter, *Unam sanctam* (1302)?

That document stated: "Outside of which [the Church] there is neither salvation nor remission of sins. . . . But we declare, state and define that to be subject to the Roman Pontiff is altogether necessary for salvation."

THE ONE-MINUTE APOLOGIST SAYS:

As with anathemas, these words are directed at other Christian churches, not individual souls, in order to make a theological point. As a point of historical fact, the Church has always painstakingly defended the valid workings of grace in non-Catholic churches. German theologian Karl Adam, in his 1924 book, *The Spirit of Catholicism*, elaborates on these questions:

To begin with, it is certain that the declaration that there is no salvation outside the Church is not aimed at individual non-Catholics, at any persons as persons, but at non-Catholic churches and communions. . . . Its purpose is to formulate positively the truth that there is but one Body of Christ and therefore but one Church which possesses and imparts the grace of Christ in its fullness.

Wherever the Gospel of Jesus is faithfully preached, and wherever baptism is conferred with faith in His Holy Name, there His grace can operate. . . . The Church . . . upheld the validity of baptism in the Name of Jesus conferred by heretics [the fourth-century Donatists]. And it was Rome, Rome that is so violently attacked for her intolerance, and Pope Stephen, who . . . would not allow heretical baptism to be impugned.

"Non-Catholic Christians know Christ, but they do not know His Church. In their desire to serve Him, they implicitly desire to be members of his Church."

FR. RAY RYLAND

[1]Acts 10:1-4

The Bible says nothing of a third state besides heaven and hell

The Catholic idea of purgatory holds people in bondage, so that they lose the joy of salvation.

THE ONE-MINUTE APOLOGIST SAYS:
The Bible actually tells us quite a bit about purgatory,
and the notion is consistent with the strong biblical themes
of divine chastisement and the sinlessness of all who enter heaven.

It's an extremely serious business to meet God face-to-face.[1] In order to stand in his presence we must be thoroughly cleansed of actual sin.[2] All Christians agree on that much. But whereas Protestants think this all occurs in an instant, Catholics think it will be a process, more like our life on earth. We are saved by God's grace and, after death, on our way to heaven. But before we get there, we must be fully sanctified by purgatorial suffering.

The souls in purgatory are spirits without bodies, so this suffering is not physical torture, but rather, a spiritual, "mental" chastisement from God (this is a very common biblical theme[3]) in order to purify and make holy and fit for heaven. It involves an intense, sorrowful anguish over the sin we have committed in our lives, and the painful desire to attain the holiness which God has called us to.[4] But the suffering will be accompanied also by great joy and hope: for heaven awaits.

Childbirth may be a useful analogy by which to understand purgatory: it involves tremendous agony, yet with a certain anticipatory acceptance even during the worst suffering, and an ecstatic joy following upon the birth. That's how it will feel after emerging from purgatory finally clean and gazing upon our Lord's beautiful and glorious face. There will not be a moment's doubt then as to whether the preparatory suffering was worth it or not.[5] We suffer much in this life, yet we also can have Christian joy.

A PROTESTANT MIGHT FURTHER OBJECT:

But Christ suffered for us! If we die in Him, we enter into heavenly bliss with no more suffering required.

This is why biblical proof for the existence of purgatory is so hard to find. It's an unbiblical tradition of men.

THE ONE-MINUTE APOLOGIST SAYS:

They are only difficult to find for those who have never been shown them, or who are taught to interpret certain verses in a different way. The Bible has a lot of indications of purgatory, either directly, or in descriptions of virtually the same process. The clearest, most indisputable passage along these lines is 1 Corinthians 3:13-15:

> [E]ach man's work will become manifest; for the Day will disclose it, because it will be revealed with fire, and the fire will test what sort of work each one has done. If the work which any man has built on the foundation survives, he will receive a reward. If any man's work is burned up, he will suffer loss, though he himself will be saved, but only as through fire.

Thus there will be some sort of suffering and judgment, even for the saved and the elect, for whom Christ died, in order that they may be made fit for heaven. It's in the Bible: Catholics didn't make it up. "Saved, but only through fire" sums up and contains the essential aspect of the concept and state of purgatory. 2 Corinthians 5:10 offers similar evidence: "For we must all appear before the judgment seat of Christ, so that each one may receive good or evil."[6]

Other passages are more indirect, yet also show that "judgment" of those who are saved, or the "righteous," is a perfectly biblical, normal thing. For example, in Psalm 66:10-12 the writer informs us that "God hast tested us; Thou hast tried us as silver is tried. . . . Thou didst lay affliction on our loins . . . we went through fire and through water." Isaiah 4:4 depicts God having "washed away the filth of the daughters of Zion and cleansed the bloodstains of Jerusalem from its midst by a spirit of judgment and by a spirit of burning."[7]

Note how Micah 7:9 also combines an assurance of salvation ("deliverance") with the willingness and necessity of suffering: "I will bear the indignation of the LORD because I have sinned against Him. . . . He will bring me forth to the light; I shall behold His deliverance." Other passages give a general portrayal of God as like a fire: not a destructive fire, but rather, a purifying force:

> **Malachi 3:2-3:** "But who can endure the day of his coming, and who can stand when he appears? 'For he is like a refiner's fire and like fullers' soap; he will sit as a refiner and purifier of silver, and he will purify the sons of Levi and refine them like gold and silver.'"[8]

Therefore, we conclude that the notion of purifying suffering after death, or purgatory, is a quite biblical concept, with many (more than enough), not few, indications.

✠

*"The foundation of the medieval doctrine is found in St. Augustine,
who holds that the fate of the individual soul is decided immediately after
death, and teaches the absolute certainty of purifying pains in the next life."*

THE OXFORD DICTIONARY OF THE CHRISTIAN CHURCH

[1]Is. 6:1-7 [2]Heb. 12:14, Rev. 21:27, 22:3, 14-15 [3]Prov. 3:11-12, Heb. 12:7-11, Jas. 1:2-4, 12, 1 Pet. 1:6-7 [4]1 Thess. 4:3, 7, 1 Jn. 3:2-9 [5]cf. Rom. 8:18 [6]cf. 7:1 [7]cf. 1:25 [8]cf. Num. 31:23, Deut. 4:24, Heb. 12:29

Our sufferings have nothing to do with those of Jesus

How could we add anything to Christ's sacrifice?
Besides, we know that He suffered so we wouldn't have to.

THE ONE-MINUTE APOLOGIST SAYS:
*Holy and meritorious suffering — with Christ and
for Him — is a prominent theme in the New Testament.*

The apostle Paul thought that his own sufferings were in some mysterious sense
joined with those of Jesus, on behalf of others; capable of an intercessory effect just
as prayer is. Biblical evidences for this are abundant:

2 Corinthians 4:10: "[A]lways carrying in the body the death of Jesus, so
that the life of Jesus may also be manifested in our bodies."[1]

Galatians 2:20: "I have been crucified with Christ; it is no longer I who
live, but Christ who lives in me; and the life I now live in the flesh I live
by faith in the Son of God, who loved me and gave Himself for me."[2]

Philippians 2:17: "Even if I am to be poured as a libation upon the sacrificial offering of your faith, I am glad and rejoice with you all."[3]

Philippians 3:8, 10-12: "Indeed I count everything as loss because of the
surpassing worth of knowing Christ Jesus my Lord. For His sake I have
suffered the loss of all things, and count them as refuse, in order that I
may gain Christ . . . and may share His sufferings, becoming like Him in
His death, that if possible I may attain the resurrection from the dead.
Not that I have already obtained this or am already perfect; but I press on
to make it my own, because Christ Jesus has made me His own."[4]

Colossians 1:24: "Now I rejoice in my sufferings for your sake, and in my
flesh I complete what is lacking in Christ's afflictions for the sake of His
body, that is, the church."

A PROTESTANT MIGHT FURTHER OBJECT:
Perhaps Paul had a special mission of suffering, but that doesn't mean we all do. Paul
was a holy man and an apostle. We're not all meant to follow his example of suffering
and martyrdom. That wouldn't be consistent with God's love for us.

The One-Minute Apologist Says:

To the contrary, St. Paul and others teach that we, too, should embrace suffering on Christ's behalf, as a normal, expected aspect of the Christian life. In a striking passage, he writes that we can be "fellow heirs with Christ" on the following condition: "provided we suffer with Him in order that we may also be glorified with Him."[5] He says that "we rejoice in our sufferings" because they produce endurance, character, and hope.[6] Jesus taught that we should rejoice when we are "persecuted for righteousness' sake . . . for your reward is great in heaven."[7] Paul taught that we should "suffer for His [Jesus'] sake,"[8] "share in suffering for the gospel in the power of God,"[9] and "If we have died with Him, we shall also live with Him."[10]

Indeed, he warns that these sufferings will come whether we like it or not, for "all who desire to live a godly life in Christ Jesus will be persecuted."[11] He was himself well-acquainted with suffering: "For the sake of Christ, then, I am content with weaknesses, insults, hardships, persecutions, and calamities; for when I am weak, then I am strong,"[12] and urges that "no one be moved by these afflictions. You yourselves know that this is to be our lot."[13]

Another beautiful passage wonderfully sums up St. Paul's teaching here:

2 Corinthians 1:5-7: "For as we share abundantly in Christ's sufferings, so through Christ we share abundantly in comfort, too. If we are afflicted, it is for your comfort and salvation; and if we are comforted, it is for your comfort, which you experience when you patiently endure the same sufferings that we suffer. Our hope for you is unshaken; for we know that as you share in our sufferings, you will also share in our comfort."

St. Peter teaches likewise:

1 Peter 4:1, 12-13, 16: "Since therefore Christ suffered in the flesh, arm yourselves with the same thought. . . . [D]o not be surprised at the fiery ordeal which comes upon you to prove you, as though something strange were happening to you. But rejoice in so far as you share Christ's sufferings . . . if one suffers as a Christian, let him not be ashamed, but under that name let him glorify God.[14]

So the Bible clearly teaches that suffering is an expected part of Christian life, not confined to saints or heroic figures. Many people understandably don't want to accept this teaching, so it is minimized or ignored. But it is undeniably a frequent biblical theme.

☩

"We all suffer for each other, and gain by each other's sufferings;
for man never stands alone here, though he will stand
by himself one day hereafter; but here he is a social being,
and goes forward to his long home as one of a large company."

John Henry Newman

---

[1]cf. 6:4-10, 11:23-30 [2]cf. 1 Cor. 15:30-31 [3]cf. 2 Tim. 2:10, 4:6 [4]cf. Gal. 6:17
[5]Rom. 8:17; cf. 8:13, 18 [6]Rom. 5:3-4 [7]Mt. 5:10, 12 [8]Phil. 1:29 [9]2 Tim. 1:8
[10]2:11 [11]3:12 [12]2 Cor. 12:10 [13]1 Thess. 3:3 [14]cf. 1:6-7, 2:20-21, 3:14, 17, 5:9-10

Theology of God

God is not three-in-one, as in the irrational doctrine of the Trinity

The Trinity is not a biblical doctrine;
it was made up by some people in the early Church.

THE ONE-MINUTE APOLOGIST SAYS:
The Christian doctrine of the Trinity, that there are three Divine Persons yet one God, is indeed taught in the Bible, albeit in seminal form.

The Holy Trinity is ultimately a deep mystery, impossible for the human mind to comprehend. Yet God undeniably reveals Himself this way in the Bible. Many scriptural passages mention all three Divine Persons,[1] but the most direct biblical evidence for the Holy Trinity is found in those passages of Holy Scripture where God the Father, Jesus the Son, and the Holy Spirit are all called God, and are all described as possessing the same properly divine attributes, such as eternity, power, glory, and so forth. Here are a few examples:

Who raised Jesus from the dead?

The Father: Galatians 1:1; cf.1 Thessolonians 1:10

The Holy Spirit: Romans 8:11

Jesus Christ: John 10:17-18; cf. 2:9

Who dwells in believers?

The Father: 1 Corinthians 3:16-17

The Holy Spirit: John 14:16-17, Romans 8:9, 1 Corinthians 2:12, 3:16, 6:19

The Son, Jesus: John 14:18, 20, 15:4, 17:23, 1 John 3:24

The Father and the Holy Spirit: 1 John 3:24, 4:12-16

The Father and the Son, Jesus: John 14:23

The Holy Spirit and the Son, Jesus: Romans 8:10, Galatians 4:6

Who searches minds and hearts?

The Father: Jeremiah 17:10

The Holy Spirit: 1 Corinthians 2:10

The Son, Jesus: Revelation 2:23

A PROTESTANT MIGHT FURTHER OBJECT:

But many biblical passages suggest that the Father is *greater* than the Son, which disproves the Trinity. For example, John 14:28: "[T]he Father is greater than I." There's also 1 Corinthians 11:3: "[T]he head of Christ is God," and 1 Corinthians 15:28: "When all things are subjected to Him, then the Son Himself will also be subjected to Him who put all things under Him, that God may be everything to every one."

THE ONE-MINUTE APOLOGIST SAYS:

John 14:28 is to be understood in light of passages such as Philippians 2:6-8; it shows us that Christ in John 14:28 was speaking strictly in terms of His office as Messiah, which entailed a temporary giving up of certain divine prerogatives (Jesus "emptied Himself, taking the form of a servant . . . humbled Himself . . ."). Christ subjected Himself to the Father in order to undertake His role as the Incarnate Son and Mediator between God and man.[2] But Jesus remains God, even while "humbling" Himself by becoming a man. Indeed, that He had to lower Himself to become man implies that Jesus was divine.

Scripture also indicates that the Father is, in a certain sense, "subject" to the Son:

> **John 16:15:** "All that the Father has is mine; therefore I said that He will take what is mine and declare it to you."[3]

In 1 Corinthians 11:3, the Father is indeed called the "head" of the Son, but this is to be understood in the same sense in which the Bible tells wives to be submissive to their husbands,[4] even though the two are equals,[5] and indeed, "one flesh."[6] Luke 2:51 even says that Jesus was "subject" to Mary and Joseph. Besides, submissiveness or servanthood is not presented as a sign of inferiority in Scripture:

> **Matthew 23:11:** "He who is greatest among you shall be your servant."[7]

The Greek word for "greatest" is *meizon*, also used in John 14:28. Moreover, in 1 Corinthians 15:28, the subjection spoken of is that of the Son as incarnate. But this is not inequality, since Colossians 3:11 proclaims: "Christ is all, and in all."

✝

"We must remind ourselves that Christian theology does not believe God to be a person. It believes Him to be such that in Him a trinity of persons is consistent with a unity of deity. In that sense it believes Him to be something very different from a person, just as a cube, in which six squares are consistent with a unity of the body, is different from a square.

"(Flatlanders, attempting to imagine a cube, would either imagine the six squares coinciding, and thus destroy their distinctness, or else imagine them set out side by side, and thus destroy the unity. Our difficulties about the Trinity are of much the same kind.)"

C. S. LEWIS

[1]Mt. 28:19, Jn. 14:26, 15:26, 16:13-15, 1 Jn. 5:7-8 [2]1 Tim. 2:5 [3]cf. Jn. 16:23 [4]1 Pet. 3:1, 5 [5]Gal. 3:28, Eph. 5:21-22 [6]Mt. 19:5-6 [7]cf. 1 Pet. 2:18

The Holy Spirit is neither a person nor God

These false beliefs were superimposed onto the Bible by later generations of misguided Christians.

THE ONE-MINUTE APOLOGIST SAYS:
The Bible teaches in many places that the Holy Spirit is indeed God: the Third Person of the Holy Trinity.

In addition to plain statements, there are many indirect evidences, and repeated personal attributes of the Holy Spirit prove He is a person, too. Here are the clearest statements in Scripture concerning the deity of the Holy Spirit:

Acts 5:3-4: "But Peter said, 'Anani'as, why has Satan filled your heart to lie to the Holy Spirit and to keep back part of the proceeds of the land? While it remained unsold, did it not remain your own? And after it was sold, was it not at your disposal? How is it that you have contrived this deed in your heart? You have not lied to men but to God.'"

Acts 28:25-27: "So, as they disagreed among themselves, they departed, after Paul had made one statement: 'The Holy Spirit was right in saying to your fathers through Isaiah the prophet: Go to this people, and say, You shall indeed hear but never understand, and you shall indeed see but never perceive. For this people's heart has grown dull, and their ears are heavy of hearing, and their eyes they have closed; lest they should perceive with their eyes, and hear with their ears, and understand with their heart, and turn for me to heal them.'"

1 Corinthians 12:4-6, 11: "Now there are varieties of gifts, but the same Spirit; and there are varieties of service, but the same Lord; and there are varieties of working, but it is the same God who inspires them all in every one. . . . All these are inspired by one and the same Spirit, who apportions to each one individually as He wills."

2 Corinthians 3:17-18: "Now the Lord is the Spirit, and where the Spirit of the Lord is, there is freedom. And we all, with unveiled face, beholding the glory of the Lord, are being changed into his likeness from one degree of glory to another; for this comes from the Lord who is the Spirit."

Who "works" all things?

The Father: 1 Corinthians 12:6; *and* the Holy Spirit: 1 Corinthians 12:11

Who is speaking to the Churches in Revelation 2 and 3?

Jesus Christ: Revelation 12:6, cf. 1:18, 2:8; *and* the Holy Spirit: Revelation 2:7; cf. 2:11, 17, 29 and 3:6, 13, 22

Who intercedes for believers?

Jesus Christ: Romans 8:34, cf. Hebrews 7:22, 25, 1 John. 2:1; *and* the Holy Spirit: Romans 8:26-27

Who gives us words to speak?

The Father: Matthew 10:19-20; Jesus: Luke 21:14-15; *and* the Holy Spirit: Mark 13:11, cf. Luke 12:11-12, John 14:26

A Protestant Might Further Object:

It makes more sense to regard the Holy Spirit according to the way we use normal language. A "spirit" is impersonal: it refers to the power or deeper meaning of something. So the Holy Spirit is not a person; it is an impersonal force.

The One-Minute Apologist Says:

The English word "spirit" can mean an impersonal force *or* a personal being. Until recently the Third Person of the Trinity was commonly called the "Holy Ghost," which is more personal-sounding, but these days is probably too suggestive of ghouls in white sheets. But the word we use to name Him isn't the point. Scripture teaches that the Holy Spirit possesses numerous personal attributes that can't apply to an impersonal "force":

The Holy Spirit *helps* (Jn. 14:16, 26, 15:26, 16:7; Rom. 8:26; 1 Jn. 2:1); *glorifies* (Jn. 16:13-14); *can be known* (Jn. 14:17); *gives abilities* (Acts 2:4; 1 Cor. 12:7-11); *is referred to as "He"* (Jn. 14:26, 15:26, 16:7-8, 13); *loves* (Rom. 15:30); *guides* (Jn. 16:13); *comforts* (Jn. 14:26, 15:26, 16:7; Acts 9:31); *teaches* (Lk. 12:12; Jn. 14:26); *reminds* (Jn. 14:26); *bears witness* (Jn. 15:26; Acts 5:32; Rom. 8:16); *has impulses* (Jn. 16:13); *hears* (Jn. 16:13); *leads* (Mt. 4:1; Acts 8:39; Rom. 8:14); *pleads* (Rom. 8:26-27); *longs or yearns* (Jas. 4:5); *wills* (1 Cor. 12:11); *thinks* (Acts 15:25, 28); *sends* (Acts 13:4); *dispatches* (Acts 10:20); *impels* (Mk. 1:12); *speaks* (Jn. 16:13-15; Acts 8:29, 10:19, 11:12, 13:2); *forbids* (Acts 16:6-7); *appoints* (Acts 20:28); *reveals* (Lk. 2:26; 1 Cor. 2:10); *calls to ministry* (Acts 13:2); *can be lied to* (Acts 5:3-4), *blasphemed* (Mt. 12:31-32), *insulted* (Heb. 10:29), *vexed* (Is. 63:10), and *grieved* (Is. 63:10; Eph. 4:30); *strives* (Gen. 6:3); *judges* (Jn. 16:8); *prophesies* (Acts 21:11, 28:25; 1 Tim. 4:1); *has fellowship* (2 Cor. 13:14); *gives grace* (Heb. 10:29); *agrees* (1 Jn. 5:7-8); and *offers life* (2 Cor. 3:6, Rev. 22:17).

✢

"In the Spirit the Father engenders the clear image of Himself in which He is 'well pleased.' In the Spirit, Jesus receives divine truth and reflects it back to the Father. . . . This mutual exchange and autonomy in the Spirit is itself a Countenance. The Third Person who makes it possible for the One to find and possess himself completely in the Other is the Holy Spirit."

Romano Guardini (Catholic theologian)

God could not have become a man

And Jesus never claimed to be God.
The Bible teaches that Jesus is God's Son, not God Himself.

THE ONE-MINUTE APOLOGIST SAYS:
There is an abundance of biblical data supporting Christ's divinity. The only way to interpret it all consistently and without contradiction is to conclude that the Jesus of Scripture really was God.

Scripture affords us many proof texts for the divinity of Jesus. Many of these are quite clear and explicit, and could hardly be interpreted any other way. The Gospel of St. John, for example, begins by telling us, "In the beginning was the Word, and the Word was with God, and the Word was God. . . . And the Word became flesh and dwelt among us."[1] Colossians 2:9 says, "For in Him the whole fullness of deity dwells bodily." In John 20:28, Thomas exclaims to Jesus, "My Lord and my God!" and Jesus does not correct him. God the Father identifies the Son as divine in Hebrews 1:8: "But of the Son He says, 'Thy throne, O God, is for ever and ever, the righteous scepter is the scepter of Thy kingdom.'" And of course Jesus Himself says plainly, "I and the Father are one."[2] Other passages are no less striking in their implications:

John 5:18: "This was why the Jews sought all the more to kill Him, because He not only broke the sabbath but also called God his Father, making Himself equal with God."[3]

John 8:58: "Truly, truly, I say to you, before Abraham was, I am."[4]

John 10:33: "The Jews answered him, 'It is not for a good work that we stone You but for blasphemy; because You, being a man, make Yourself God.'"

Philippians 2:5-6: "Have this mind among yourselves, which is yours in Christ Jesus, who, though he was in the form of God, did not count equality with God a thing to be grasped."

Colossians 1:16-17: "For in him all things were created, in heaven and on earth, visible and invisible, whether thrones or dominions or principalities or authorities — all things were created through Him and for Him. He is before all things, and in Him all things hold together."[5]

A PROTESTANT MIGHT REPLY:

But in the Bible Jesus is called God's "only-begotten Son." He is the "first-born,"[6] and "the beginning of God's creation."[7] All of this strongly suggests that he was created, and thus could not have been the eternal God.

THE ONE-MINUTE APOLOGIST SAYS:

These are standard arguments made by Jehovah's Witnesses, Unitarians, and others who deny the orthodox Christian doctrine of the Incarnation and the deity of Jesus Christ. They have been answered many times throughout history.

The phrase "only-begotten [Son]" — used in the King James and other Bible translations — is the Greek *monogenes*, which means, according to any Greek lexicon, "unique, only member of a kind." It does not mean "created." The Nicene Creed makes this very clear:

> We believe in one Lord, Jesus Christ, the only Son of God, eternally begotten of the Father, God from God, Light from Light, true God from true God, begotten, not made, of one Being with the Father. Through Him all things were made.

Christ is the eternal Son of God, and as such, possesses every attribute of pure Godhood, just as a human son fully possesses every attribute of humanness.

The Greek word for "first-born" is *prototokos*, which means "preeminence" and "eternal preexistence," according to Greek lexicons. It does not mean "first-created." Apart from that, this heretical interpretation (as applied to Col. 1:15) is contradicted two verses later, where Paul informs us that Christ "is before all things" (eternally existent), and four verses later (1:19): "For in him all the fullness of God was pleased to dwell."

The Hebrew usage of "first-born" is also instructive, since it illustrates its meaning as "preeminent." David is called "first-born" in Ps. 89:27, not because he was the literal first child of Jesse (for he was the youngest), but in the sense of his ascendancy to the kingship of Israel. Likewise, Jeremiah 31:9 refers to Ephraim as "my first-born," whereas Manasseh was the first child born.[8] The nation Israel is called "my first-born son" by God.[9]

The Greek for "beginning" is *arche*, from which we get our word "architect." Its literal meaning, according to Greek scholars, is "origin, active cause, source, uncreated principle." So the above verse is describing Jesus as the "architect," or creator. In Revelation 21:6, *arche* is also applied to God the Father ("I am the Alpha and the Omega, the beginning and the end"), so it can't possibly mean "created being." In Revelation 1:17-18 and 22:13, Jesus calls Himself the "Alpha and Omega" and "first and last."

✛

"Rationalists renounce reason in their attempt to solve the problem of Christ. Either Christ was God or He was mad. The rationalist will not accept the former alternative; he dare not suggest the latter."

SIR ARNOLD LUNN (ENGLISH WRITER)

[1]Jn. 1:1, 14 [2]Jn. 10:30 [3]cf. 5:26 [4]cf. Ex. 3:14 [5]cf. Jn. 1:10, Heb. 1:10
[6]Col. 1:15, Heb. 1:6 [7]Rev. 3:14 [8]Gen. 41:50-52 [9]Ex. 4:22

Jesus had to grow into the understanding that He was God

He was limited in His awareness and in His learning abilities because He was a man, like the rest of us.

THE ONE-MINUTE APOLOGIST SAYS:

The confusion here comes from the fact that Jesus fully possessed two natures: divine and human. In His divine nature He was omniscient, yet in his human nature He had to learn and grow like any other human being.

Jesus had at all times the attributes of God and also those of man. He wasn't "half-and-half" with a hybrid "divine-human nature" (this is the heresy of Monophysitism), but rather, God and man simultaneously. Yet the two natures remain separate. These theological definitions are supremely important because Jesus was both God (the Second Person of the Trinity) and took on flesh to become man (in the Incarnation). Both teachings needed to be fully preserved, rather than one nature being emphasized over the other (an overemphasis on the human nature of Christ at the expense of the divine is the heresy of Nestorianism).

Omniscience (knowledge of all things) was not a characteristic of Jesus' human intellect or nature, but it was part of His divine nature. Jesus' human nature meant that He could progressively learn, just as all men do, yet at the same time in His divine nature He knew all things. The two natures unite in the Person of Jesus Christ.

Many other passages show that Jesus possessed the quality of omniscience in His divine nature, including knowing at all times that He was God; He didn't "grow" into that "consciousness":

John 16:28-30: "'I came from the Father and have come into the world; again, I am leaving the world and going to the Father.' His disciples said, 'Ah, now You are speaking plainly, not in any figure! Now we know that You know all things, and need none to question You.'"[1]

John 18:4: "Jesus, knowing all that was to befall Him."[2]

John 18:36-37: "Jesus answered, 'My kingship is not of this world; if my kingship were of this world, my servants would fight, that I might not be handed over to the Jews; but my kingship is not from the world.' Pilate said to Him, 'So you are a king?' Jesus answered, 'You say that I am a king.

For this I was born, and for this I have come into the world, to bear witness to the truth. Every one who is of the truth hears my voice.'"

John 21:17: "Lord, You know everything."[3]

Colossians 2:2-3: "Christ, in whom are hid all the treasures of wisdom and knowledge."[4]

Other passages show Jesus possessing supernatural knowledge; although not in themselves proof of omniscience, they do prove that Jesus was more than a mere man.[5]

A PROTESTANT MIGHT FURTHER OBJECT:

But some passages show that Jesus' knowledge is limited or incomplete. For example, Matthew 24:36: "But of that day and hour no one knows, not even the angels of heaven, nor the Son, but the Father only." Doesn't that prove that He wasn't omniscient?

THE ONE-MINUTE APOLOGIST SAYS:

In becoming man, Jesus voluntarily limited Himself in His human nature — but not His divine (see Philippians 2:6-8: "though He was in the form of God, did not count equality with God a thing to be grasped, but emptied Himself, taking the form of a servant, being born in the likeness of men. And being found in human form He humbled Himself"). Matthew 24:36 simply shows Jesus speaking from His human nature, where He didn't know all things; speaking as the incarnate Son, who gave up divine prerogatives in terms of His human nature (while never losing them in His divine nature).

Besides, there are many other verses illustrating that Jesus (in His divine nature) knew the future perfectly:

Matthew 20:18-19: "Behold, we are going up to Jerusalem; and the Son of man will be delivered to the chief priests and scribes, and they will condemn Him to death, and deliver Him to the Gentiles to be mocked and scourged and crucified, and He will be raised on the third day."[6]

John 6:64: "'But there are some of you that do not believe.' For Jesus knew from the first who those were that did not believe, and who it was that would betray Him."

(See also: Mt. 12:40, 17:9, 11-12, 22-23, 21:39, 24:2, 26:2, 12, 21, 31-34, 54; Mk. 8:31, 9:31, 10:32-34, 14:9, 18, 27-30, 42, 49; Lk. 9:22, 44, 11:30, 12:50, 17:25, 22:15, 21-22, 32, 34, 37; Jn. 2:19, 3:14, 10:11, 15, 17-18, 12:32-34, 13:18-21, 14:19, 15:13, 16:20, 18:11.)

✝

"Both divine and human attributes can be predicated of him, although the two natures are separated by an infinite abyss. I can say that Christ is omniscient (as God), but also that he does not know everything (as man); God is lying in the crib (that is, as a man); God is dying on the cross. . . ."

MATTHIAS PREMM (CATHOLIC THEOLOGIAN)

[1]cf. Mt. 6:8 [2]cf. Acts 15:18 [3]cf. 1 Jn. 3:20 [4]cf. Rom. 11:33-34 [5]Mt. 9:4, 12:25, Mk. 2:8, Lk. 6:8, 9:47, 22:10-13, Jn. 6:64, 13:1, 10-11 [6]cf. 16:21, Lk. 18:31-33

Mary and the Saints

Mary was not sinless
throughout her whole life

The Bible says everyone has sinned, and
that Mary needed a savior just like the rest of us.

THE ONE-MINUTE APOLOGIST SAYS:
*Through the grace of the sacrifice of our Lord and Savior
Jesus Christ on the Cross, Mary was preserved from original sin
and its effects. This is the doctrine of the Immaculate Conception.*

Romans 3:23 ("since all have sinned and fall short of the glory of God") is very commonly cited as an objection to Mary's sinlessness. And in her *Magnificat*,[1] she indeed describes God as her "savior." But Catholics don't see her as an exception to the universal human need for salvation. Mary certainly would have been subject to original sin and its effects — were it not for God's extraordinary act of grace. Therefore, God is her Savior too, but in a *prevenient* way.

To illustrate this doctrine, the medieval theologians argued that a person walking through the woods near a hidden pit could be "saved" from it in two different ways: by being warned so that they avoid falling into it, or (having fallen in) by being rescued from it. The first example applies to Mary; the latter applies to all of us who inherited original sin. In both cases, however, salvation must come through God's grace alone. Mary could no more save herself than we can. The Immaculate Conception is as much pure grace as is possible.

The meanings of words in the Hebrew language were somewhat fluid, and Hebrew poetry and everyday language very often used exaggeration to emphasize some truth. Recognizing this, most Christians would hold that very young children are not capable of committing actual sin. In the same book of Romans, St. Paul states that "all Israel will be saved,"[2] but we know that many will not be saved. And in 15:14, the apostle describes members of the Roman church as "filled with all knowledge" (clearly not literally true).

Note also Paul's proclamation in 1 Corinthians 15:22: "For as in Adam all die, so also in Christ shall all be made alive." Not "all" people have physically died.[3] Likewise, "all" will not be made spiritually alive by Christ, as some will suffer eternal spiritual death in hell. These are clearly poetic generalizations. Many other similar examples can be found. We observe the same dynamic in the Psalms:

Psalm 14:2-3: "The LORD looks down from heaven upon the children of men, to see if there are any that act wisely, that seek after God. They have all gone astray, they are all alike corrupt; there is none that does good, no, not one."[4]

Yet in the very next chapter David refers to him "who walks blamelessly, and does what is right."[5] Two verses after the above passage[6] he writes that "God is with the generation of the righteous." Obviously, then, his lament in 14:2-3 is not intended as a literal utterance. The book of Proverbs repeatedly refers to the "good" or "righteous" man.[7] And references to righteous or holy men are simply innumerable. Therefore, Romans 3:23 alone cannot possibly disprove the Blessed Virgin Mary's sinlessness (or her Immaculate Conception).

A PROTESTANT MIGHT FURTHER OBJECT:

Still, this explanation does not *prove* by direct statements from the Bible that Mary was actually sinless.

Since the Fall, all men have been subject to original sin, and that must include Mary. Otherwise, she becomes a goddess-like figure; we ascribe to her attributes that only God possesses.

THE ONE-MINUTE APOLOGIST SAYS:

It's true that the biblical arguments alone above do not prove Mary's sinlessness; however, they do demonstrate the inadequacy of the prooftexts for her alleged sinfulness, and show how the Bible does not regard sinlessness as an impossible or unattainable state.

Positive biblical proof, moreover, is found in Luke 1:28: "Hail, O favored one, the Lord is with you!" The Greek word for "favored one" is *kecharitomene*. Baptist Greek scholar A.T. Robertson defines it as "endowed with grace" or "full of grace which thou hast received."[8] Since we are saved by grace alone,[9] and since grace is the vanquisher and opposite of sin (Romans 5:17; also 6:14: "For sin will have no dominion over you, since you are not under law but under grace"), to be "full" of grace is to be without sin.

Sinlessness is not a quality of God alone, because Adam and Eve before the Fall were sinless, and all the unfallen angels are so now. Explicit biblical proof is an unreasonable requirement of the unbiblical tradition of *sola Scriptura*.

✠

"We must except the holy Virgin Mary, concerning whom I wish to raise
no question when it touches the subject of sins, out of honor to the Lord;
for from Him we know what abundance of grace for overcoming sin
in every particular was conferred upon her who had the merit to
conceive and bear Him who undoubtedly had no sin."

ST. AUGUSTINE

[1]Lk. 1:47 [2]11:26 [3]e.g., Enoch: Gen. 5:24; cf. Heb 11:5; Elijah: 2 Kings 2:11
[4]cf. 53:1-3, Rom. 3:10-12 [5]15:2 [6]14:5 [7]e.g., 11:23, 12:2, 13:22, 14:14, 19
[8]*Word Pictures in the New Testament* [9]Eph. 2:8, Rom. 3:24, Titus 2:11

Mary had other children besides Jesus

The Bible often refers to "brothers" of Jesus. This proves Mary did not remain a virgin.

THE ONE-MINUTE APOLOGIST SAYS:
"Brothers" in Scripture signifies a wide range of kinship and other relationships, so the word by itself proves nothing.

A great deal of internal biblical proof also suggests that Jesus had no siblings, which is why even Luther and Calvin agreed with the Catholic position. Biblical examples of the word "brothers" signifying something other than "siblings" are numerous: nationality,[1] a neighbor,[2] those with a common interest[3] or calling,[4] all mankind,[5] disciples,[6] all Christians,[7] and so forth. This wide usage occurs in both Hebrew and Greek (and, for that matter, also in English).

The Hebrews also commonly used the word "brother" to mean the generic "relative." James and Joseph are described in Matthew 13:55 (along with Simon and Jude) as Jesus' "brothers." But they are also called sons of Mary, wife of Clopas.[8] (Mary is called the Blessed Virgin Mary's "sister";[9] this suggests that she was a cousin or other kind of non-sibling relative, since two siblings would not likely both be named Mary). Elsewhere,[10] Simon, Jude, James, Joseph, and "sisters" are all described with the same Greek word as all the above examples *(adelphoi)*. Since we know from the above that James and Joseph are not Jesus' blood brothers, the most sensible interpretation of the word in Matthew 13:55 is "cousins."

Of the other two named "brothers" of Jesus, Jude identifies himself in the beginning of his letter as "a servant of Jesus Christ and brother of James," which would be exceedingly strange if he were, in fact, the blood brother of Jesus our Lord. So it is far more likely that he was a blood brother of James and a cousin of Jesus. As for the fourth "brother," Simon, or Symeon, second-century historian Hegesippus, as cited by Eusebius, states that he was also a son of Clopas, making him a cousin of Jesus. That plausibly accounts for all four as cousins.

In Luke 2:41-51, the twelve-year-old Jesus is described as being taken to the Temple, but His supposed several siblings are nowhere to be found in the narrative. Nor do we see them at the foot of the Cross, where Jesus gives His mother to the care of the Beloved Disciple[11] — not to one of His alleged brothers.

Catholics are often asked why this doctrine is so important. Apart from its simply being (as Catholics and many other Christians believe) what the Bible teaches, one reason is its preservation of the doctrine of the virgin birth, and hence, indirectly, the Incarnation. If Mary had had other children in the usual way, then everyone would know she had conceived children by natural means, and the potential would exist to deny that Jesus' birth was supernatural. Her remaining a virgin her entire life underscores the extraordinary miracle of Jesus' conception.

A Protestant Might Further Object:

But besides the strong evidence of "brothers" in Scripture we also have the evidence of Matthew 1:24-25: "Joseph . . . took his wife, but knew her not until she had borne a Son, and he called His name Jesus."

This proves that Joseph and Mary had normal marital relations after the birth of Jesus. Also, Matthew 1:18 teaches us that Joseph and Mary eventually "came together" — which means conjugal relations.

The One-Minute Apologist Says:

The word "until" doesn't necessarily imply a change in a state of affairs. In both English grammar and biblical usage it can simply mean "up to the time of." For example, Jesus says, "From the days of John the Baptist until now, the kingdom of heaven has suffered violence, and men of violence take it by force."[12] Clearly, this violence didn't cease at that time; it was ongoing. "Until" here doesn't prove that the violence ceased at the time that Jesus said this. Likewise, it is not true that Joseph must have "known" Mary after Jesus was born, simply because of the word "until." John Calvin was so sure of the same thing that he wrote:

> No just and well-grounded inference can be drawn from these words . . . as
> to what took place after the birth of Christ. He is called "first-born"; but it
> is for the sole purpose of informing us that he was born of a virgin. [13]

The Greek word for "came together" *(sunerchomai)*, has a wide range of meaning, far beyond sex. In fact, if we look at all the New Testament usages of this word, only one instance out of thirty-two is clearly sexual in meaning, in context (1 Cor. 7:5). Thirty other instances are clearly not sexual in nature: Mk. 3:20, 6:33, 14:53; Lk. 5:15, 23:55; Jn. 11:33, 18:20; Acts 1:6, 21, 2:6, 5:16, 9:39, 10:23, 27, 45, 11:12, 15:38, 16:13, 19:32, 21:16, 22, 25:17, 28:17; 1 Cor. 11:17, 18, 20, 33, 34, 14:23, 26.

☩

"A new lie about me is being circulated. I am supposed to have
preached and written that Mary, the mother of God, was not a
virgin either before or after the birth of Christ. . . . Scripture does
not say or indicate that she later lost her virginity."

Martin Luther

[1]Rom. 9:3 [2]Lk. 10:29 [3]Mt. 5:47 [4]Rev. 22:9 [5]Mt. 25:40 [6]Mt. 12:49-50, 23:1,
Jn. 20:17 [7]Rom. 1:13 [8]Matt. 27:56 with Mk. 15:40 and Jn. 19:25
[9]Jn. 19:25 [10]Mt. 13:55-56, Mk. 6:3 [11]Jn. 19:27 [12]Mt. 11:12;
cf. 1 Tim. 4:13 [13]*Harmony of Matthew, Mark and Luke*

Calling Mary the "Mother of God" makes her greater than God

This is another example of Catholicism's inventing an unbiblical tradition to raise Mary to the level of a goddess.

THE ONE-MINUTE APOLOGIST SAYS:
The title "Mother of God" (Greek, Theotokos, *or "God-bearer") refers to the indisputable fact that Mary was the mother of Jesus, who was God.*

Catholics, Orthodox, and traditional Protestants all believe that Jesus was Divinity Incarnate: God in the flesh; the Second Person of the Holy Trinity. The title of *Theotokos* was used by the early Church to protect the full doctrine of Christ's deity, since in the first few centuries some were arguing that Mary was the mother of His human nature only, thereby throwing into confusion the precise relationship between Jesus' divine and human natures.

For it would be odd to say that human mothers give birth only to a "body" or a "nature"; they give birth to human persons with both body and soul. Likewise, Mary gave birth to Jesus as a person both human and divine (even though she had nothing to do with His divine nature, which existed eternally). To deny that she gave birth to "the man who was God" is effectively to deny the fundamental Christian doctrine of the hypostatic union — the substantial, unmixed, unseparated union of two natures in the one person of Jesus Christ.

And so Mary is rightly called "Mother of God," a title that is as much about Jesus as it is about her. It does not make her some kind of goddess; Mary did not bring divinity into being. Only sheer misunderstanding and anti-Catholic animus would have the title mean any more than it does. Virtually all of the early Protestant leaders (including John Calvin) continued to use the term.

It should hardly be necessary to prove to most Christians that Mary was Jesus' mother, and that Jesus was God the Son, Second Person of the Holy Trinity. She is called "the mother of Jesus";[1] "His mother" or "Mary His mother,"[2] and "mother of my Lord."[3] Also, the familiar Christmas passage explicitly teaches the same thing:

> **Luke 1:31-35:** "And behold, you will conceive in your womb and bear a Son, and you shall call His name Jesus. He will be great, and will be called the Son of the Most High; and the Lord God will give to Him the throne of His father David, and He will reign over the house of Jacob for ever; and of His

kingdom there will be no end. And Mary said to the angel, 'How shall this be, since I have no husband?' And the angel said to her, 'The Holy Spirit will come upon you, and the power of the Most High will overshadow you; therefore the child to be born will be called holy, the Son of God.'"[4]

To the objection of non-trinitarians that "Son of God" suggests "lesser than God" or a creature, rather than (literally) God the Son, a decisive biblical reply is found in the Gospel of John. Jesus has all of the attributes of divinity and Godhood. He does everything the Father does, has power over life and death, judges mankind, and is honored equally with God the Father:

> **John 5:19-23, 26-27:** "Jesus said to them, 'Truly, truly, I say to you, the Son can do nothing of His own accord, but only what He sees the Father doing; for whatever He does, that the Son does likewise. For the Father loves the Son, and shows Him all that He Himself is doing; and greater works than these will He show Him, that you may marvel. For as the Father raises the dead and gives them life, so also the Son gives life to whom He will. . . . For as the Father has life in Himself, so He has granted the Son also to have life in Himself, and has given Him authority to execute judgment, because He is the Son of man.'"[5]

A PROTESTANT MIGHT FURTHER OBJECT:

But Catholics nonetheless take this title too far. In the context of all their excessive Marian doctrines and devotions, Catholics clearly exalt Mary far higher than the way she is presented in Scripture: as a humble handmaiden of the Lord.

THE ONE-MINUTE APOLOGIST SAYS:

God the Father, not the Catholic Church, chose to use Mary in the Incarnation. How is it possible for Catholics to honor and revere her any more than God already has, by choosing her to bear and raise His Son? God made her "blessed among women," and Catholics simply do their best to recognize that fact.

All of the honors accorded to Mary ultimately point to Jesus. Giving her the title "Mother of God" safeguards the truth of the Incarnation. It reaffirms that Jesus is God as well as man. It highlights His unique position as the God-Man, the Incarnate God, just as the virgin birth shows that He was absolutely special: miraculously conceived because the Incarnation itself was a one-of-a-kind supernatural occurrence.

✝

"She became the Mother of God . . . on this there follows all honor,
all blessedness, and her unique place in the whole of mankind,
among which she has no equal, namely, that she had a child by the
Father in heaven, and such a Child. . . . Hence men have crowded
all her glory into a single word, calling her the Mother of God."

MARTIN LUTHER

[1]Jn. 2:1 [2]Mt. 1:18, 2:11, 13, 20, 12:46, 13:55 [3]Lk. 1:43
[4]cf. Is. 7:14, Gal. 4:4 [5]cf. Jn. 10:33

Mary could not have been "assumed" into heaven

The Bible doesn't give any indication
at all for this, so why do Catholics believe it?

THE ONE-MINUTE APOLOGIST SAYS:
Although no explicit biblical evidence for it exists,
Mary's bodily Assumption is not contrary to anything in the Bible,
and it makes perfect sense, given that she was the mother of our Lord.

It is important to recognize the difference between "unbiblical" (meaning completely absent from the Bible, or contradictory to it) and "not explicitly found in the Bible." To claim, for example, "God had a beginning and He doesn't know the future" is a blatant contradiction of biblical teaching and so must be rejected by all who believe that the Bible is inspired revelation. But to say, "Mary was bodily assumed into heaven" is not contrary to any biblical teaching. Rather, Scripture simply doesn't address it. Since the Bible nowhere says that all Christian truth must be contained in it, and in fact states that not all truth is found in it,[1] this should not alarm anyone.

But it is reasonable to ask why Catholics believe in this doctrine at all, and on what grounds. The Catholic outlook here is fairly simple: Adam and Eve were created without sin. They never had to sin, but they chose to rebel against God's commands and authority, so consequently the human race fell and all human beings are ordinarily subject to death and decay as a result.[2] Mary, on the other hand, was given the great gift of being conceived without the taint of Adam and Eve's sin, so that she never committed actual sin. She received this gift because she was to be the mother of the Second Person of the Trinity, and God thought it was fitting to prepare a pure and unspoiled vessel for Him. Her condition represented what all human beings could and would have been, and what saved persons one day will be: without sin.

Since she was without sin, and thus didn't have to die or undergo the decay of death, at the time of God's choosing she was assumed bodily into heaven (which is different from ascending to heaven under one's own power, as Jesus did). Jesus' Resurrection made possible the eventual bodily resurrection of all of his followers,[3] and Mary was the first to enjoy the reward made available to all who would believe in Him. After all, what is more appropriate than that Jesus' own mother should be blessed in such a way? She brought Him into this world, and so He brought her in a special way into the next world, body and soul. She represents the coming of the Kingdom, including new bodies and the end of death and sin.[4]

A Protestant Might Further Object:

It might be possible to believe something if it is not expressly taught in the Bible, as long as it is not contrary to overall biblical teaching, or can at least be logically deduced or derived from clear Scripture. But there is nothing even remotely indicative of the Assumption in the Bible. It seems to be a doctrine invented out of whole cloth.

The One-Minute Apologist Says:

Catholics readily admit that no explicit biblical support for the Assumption exists; yet there are indeed biblical indications of a special or extraordinary death, or "visit to heaven" in a way out of the ordinary.

For example, the early biblical figure Enoch was a particularly righteous man. It is written that he "walked with God" and that "he was not, for God took him."[5] This description is somewhat mysterious, but New Testament revelation further explains it:

> **Hebrews 11:5**: "By faith Enoch was taken up so that he should not see death; and he was not found, because God had taken him. Now before he was taken he was attested as having pleased God."

Nor is this the only such instance. The Apostle Paul writes about being "caught up to the third heaven" before he died,[6] possibly bodily ("whether in the body or out of the body I do not know"). In 1 Thessalonians 4:15-17, Paul teaches that those who are alive when Jesus comes again to earth, will (apparently) not experience death: "We who are alive, who are left, shall be caught up together with them in the clouds to meet the Lord in the air; and so we shall always be with the Lord."

Of course, the most extraordinary biblical example of an "entrance into the next life" is that of the great prophet Elijah:

> **2 Kings 2:11**: "And as they still went on and talked, behold, a chariot of fire and horses of fire separated the two of them. And Eli'jah went up by a whirlwind into heaven."

☩

"Elijah was transported body and soul in a chariot of fire; he was not buried in any Church bearing his name, but mounted up to heaven, so that . . . we might know what immortality and recompense God prepares for his faithful prophets and for his most outstanding and incomparable creatures. . . . It is for this reason, we believe, that the pure and immaculate embodiment of the Mother of God, the Virgin Mary, the Temple of the Holy Spirit, that is to say her saintly body, was carried up to heaven by the angels."

Heinrich Bullinger (prominent early Protestant leader)

[1]Jn. 20:30, 21:25 [2]Gen. 3:19, Ps. 16:10 [3]1 Cor. 15:13-16
[4]1 Cor. 15:26 [5]Gen. 5:24 [6]2 Cor. 12:2-4

Calling Mary the "Mediatrix" of graces makes her equal to Jesus

Jesus Christ is the *sole* mediator between God and man. Once again the Catholic Church unduly exalts Mary and detracts from the glory of her Son.

THE ONE-MINUTE APOLOGIST SAYS:

If God desired to use Mary or anyone else as an intermediary for His saving grace, He could certainly do so; in fact there are many indications of such things in Scripture, and nothing proving it's impossible.

In becoming man and coming to earth, God chose to involve a human being: Mary. He didn't have to do so; He could have simply appeared as a grown man, as Adam had. But it pleased God to involve human "mediation" in the Incarnation, by enlisting the cooperation of Mary and human biology. So Mary is Mediatrix in that first sense — she brought Jesus into the world, which in turn led to our salvation.

Moreover, just as we are allowed the unfathomable privilege of participating (in a certain limited sense) in our own redemption and cooperating with God,[1] all by His grace, likewise God willed that the Blessed Virgin Mary would play a part in the redemption of all, by consenting to the sacrifice of her Son on the Cross. She didn't cause the redemption any more than we cause our own redemption. It doesn't raise her to the level of God in any way, shape, or form. All it means is that God chose to use her in an extraordinary way for His will.

This was God's marvelous plan for salvation: to involve a creature — a woman — at every step of the way. Eve brought down the human race, acting with Adam; Mary (the "second Eve," as many Church Fathers called her) helped to raise it, acting in concert with Jesus Christ, her Son, the second Adam (see 1 Corinthians 15:45).

Nothing in these concepts is contrary to Scripture or Tradition. God clearly uses human beings as mediators. God could even use Mary as a channel in distributing His grace to mankind, as Catholics believe.

God used a donkey ("Balaam's ass") to speak and express His will once.[2] He appeared in a burning bush.[3] He told Isaiah to walk around naked for three years,[4] and to compare men's actions to menstrual rags (the literal meaning of Isaiah 64:6). Why should anything He does surprise us? His thoughts are as far above ours as the stars are above the earth.[5] As with the Assumption, there is no direct biblical proof of this, but there are many indications of something highly similar to Mary being a mediatrix in terms of God's grace given to human beings.

A PROTESTANT MIGHT FURTHER OBJECT:

But all we have to do is believe that Jesus died for us, and we are saved — see John 1:29 and 3:16). To deny that is to say that Jesus' death wasn't good enough to save us!

THE ONE-MINUTE APOLOGIST SAYS:

The Bible provides examples of God's enabling and using His creatures — even for the purpose of helping to save others and bring them grace. In fact, it's rather common. For example, we see Moses saying to his people, "Now I will go up to the LORD; perhaps I can make atonement for your sin,"[6] and St. Paul exclaiming, "I have become all things to all men, that I might by all means save some."[7] We know that it technically wasn't Paul who "saved" anyone; it was God. In the same manner, Catholics know that Mary doesn't save anyone when God uses her as a vessel to distribute His grace.

Paul elsewhere explains more clearly the relationship between God's grace and God's use of him as a vessel, referring to "the stewardship of God's grace that was given to me for you."[8] He urges, "Take heed to yourself and to your teaching; hold to that, for by so doing you will save both yourself and your hearers"[9] and "Let no evil talk come out of your mouths, but only such as is good for edifying, as fits the occasion, that it may impart grace to those who hear."[10] Note these extraordinary passages also:

> **2 Corinthians 4:10-12, 15**: "[A]lways carrying in the body the death of Jesus, so that the life of Jesus may also be manifested in our bodies. For while we live we are always being given up to death for Jesus' sake, so that the life of Jesus may be manifested in our mortal flesh. So death is at work in us, but life in you. . . . For it is all for your sake, so that as grace extends to more and more people it may increase thanksgiving, to the glory of God."[11]

> **Revelation 1:4**: "John to the seven churches that are in Asia: Grace to you and peace from Him who is and who was and who is to come, and from the seven spirits who are before His throne."

All of this indicates that God uses human "mediators" as conveyors of His saving grace. This doesn't detract from the unique mediation of Jesus Christ, but rather depends on it. Mary's role is simply the most extraordinary example of God's "method" in saving His creatures.

✛

"He wills indeed according to her prayer, but then she prays according to His will. Though then it is natural and prudent for those to have recourse to her, who from the Church's teaching know her power."

JOHN HENRY NEWMAN

[1]Phil. 2:12-13 [2]Num. 22:30 [3]Ex. 3:2-4 [4]Is. 20:2-4 [5]Is. 55:8-9 [6]Ex. 32:30 [7]1 Cor. 9:22 [8]Eph. 3:2; cf. 2 Cor. 6:1, 1 Pet. 4:10, 2 Pet. 1:2 [9]1 Tim. 4:16 [10]Eph. 4:29; cf. Jas. 4:6 [11]cf. 2 Cor. 11:23-30, Gal. 6:17, Phil. 2:7, Col. 1:24, 2 Tim. 4:6

There's no reason for Christians to pray for the dead

After death comes judgment — when the dead are beyond the help of our prayers.

THE ONE-MINUTE APOLOGIST SAYS:
Prayers for the dead are solidly founded on religious and theological tradition, and on the testimony of Scripture.

Far from being a Catholic or even a Christian innovation, prayers for the dead were a normative expression of Jewish religion:

> **2 Maccabees 12:42, 44-45**: "[A]nd they turned to prayer, beseeching that the sin which had been committed might be wholly blotted out. . . . [I]f he were not expecting that those who had fallen would rise again, it would have been superfluous and foolish to pray for the dead. But if he was looking to the splendid reward that is laid up for those who fall asleep in godliness, it was a holy and pious thought. Therefore he made atonement for the dead, that they might be delivered from their sin."[1]

The apostle Paul virtually cites the middle section of this passage in his very strange (to "Protestant ears") passage on baptism for the dead:

> **1 Corinthians 15:29**: "Otherwise, what do people mean by being baptized on behalf of the dead? If the dead are not raised at all, why are people baptized on their behalf?"

Protestants will reply that 2 Maccabees is from the "Apocrypha," which is another discussion, but whether it is Scripture or not (the early Church certainly thought so), the passage still shows beyond any doubt that this was the practice of the Jews and that neither they nor the writer saw any connection at all between such prayers and forbidden practices of necromancy and divination. Christianity is a development of Judaism, which is why Jesus said, "Think not that I have come to abolish the law and the prophets; I have come . . . to fulfill them."[2]

A PROTESTANT MIGHT FURTHER OBJECT:

The books of the Apocrypha aren't Scripture, and 1 Corinthians 15:29 isn't clear enough to settle the issue. What we really need is a plain statement in the New Testament that prayers for the dead are permissible, and we simply don't see that.

If there is no such plain statement, there was no need for one, since praying for the dead was an understood and accepted thing in Jewish culture (and Christianity was firmly rooted in that culture and received its theology from it). But St. Paul suggests that we can not only do works on "behalf" of the dead (as in 1 Corinthians 15:29, above), but also pray for them, since he did so himself:

2 Timothy 1:16, 18: "May the Lord grant mercy to the household of Onesiph'orus . . . may the Lord grant him to find mercy from the Lord on that Day — and you well know all the service he rendered at Ephesus."

Many Protestant commentaries state that here Paul is praying for Onesiphorus, yet few of them acknowledge that he is dead (as seems fairly straightforward from the way Paul refers to him), presumably to avoid the embarrassing inference that would follow. But Catholics are free to believe both things and accept the natural reading. Paul isn't trying to "conjure up" anyone, as in occultic practices; he is simply praying for them.

All Christians believe that those who die in Christ (the saved, the elect) are still alive. If one believes that the person who dies goes straight to hell or heaven, with no intermediate or transitional state, then praying for the dead would be unnecessary and meaningless (since the damned could no longer be helped and the saved would not be in need of any further help). But this practice flows logically from the existence of purgatory. The latter (dealt with in detail in this book) is most clearly indicated in passages such as 1 Corinthians 3:13-15 and 2 Corinthians 5:10 and 7:1, among many other indirect evidences.

Therefore, since an "intermediate" condition or state of purifying suffering after death is clearly indicated in the Bible, it is perfectly acceptable and normal and praiseworthy (and biblical) to pray for people who are in this state (or deemed as likely to be so). It extends the practice of charity not only to people on the earth, but also to those loved ones who have departed the earth and are with God, but not yet in the fullest, most glorious way (when they shall see Him "face-to-face").

✙

"As for the dead, since Scripture gives us no information on the subject, I regard it as no sin to pray with free devotion in this or some similar fashion: 'Dear God, if this soul is in a condition accessible to mercy, be thou gracious to it.'"

MARTIN LUTHER

"Augustine . . . himself remembered in prayer his godly mother at her dying request."

PHILIP SCHAFF (PROTESTANT CHURCH HISTORIAN)

[1]cf. 12:39-41 (for context) [2]Mt. 5:17

Praying to saints is wrong

The Bible forbids communication
with the dead. It also tells us there is only
one mediator between God and men: Jesus.

THE ONE-MINUTE APOLOGIST SAYS:
*The Bible teaches that those who die and are saved are
fully alive, that they are aware of earthly affairs, and that they
love us; therefore it makes perfect sense to ask for their intercession.*

Protestants often ask Catholics a question that goes something like this: "Why would anyone seek the aid of a mere manager or underling, when he can go directly to the CEO himself?" The comparison is, of course, to asking saints to pray for us when we can go "straight to God." In this vein, they cite 1 Timothy 2:5 ("one mediator"). And the proper Catholic (and biblical) answer is, "Because we are informed in the Bible that the prayers of certain people are more effective than those of others":

James 5:16-18: "The prayer of a righteous man has great power in its effects. Elijah was a man of like nature with ourselves and he prayed fervently that it might not rain, and for three years and six months it did not rain on the earth. Then he prayed again and the heaven gave rain, and the earth brought forth its fruit."

This brings to mind other powerful intercessors, such as Abraham and Moses, whose pleas were so strong that they convinced God not to destroy entire cities or peoples. If, then, the Blessed Virgin Mary were indeed sinless, it would follow (right from Scripture) that her prayers would have the greatest power, and not only because of her sinlessness but because of her status as Mother of God. So we ask for her prayers and also ask other saints, because they have more power than we do, having been made perfectly righteous (according to James 5:16-18).

Most Protestants are quite comfortable asking for prayers from other Christians on earth; why do they not ask those saved saints who have departed from the earth and are close to God in heaven? After all, they may have passed from this world, but they're certainly alive — more than we are! Jesus alludes to this fact when He speaks of "the God of Abraham, Isaac, and Jacob," stating that "He is not God of the dead, but of the living."[1] And those in heaven no longer have any sin.[2]

If it is objected that the dead saints cannot hear us, we reply that God is fully able to give them that power — with plenty of supporting biblical evidence: 1) the "cloud of witnesses" that Hebrews 12:1 describes; 2) in Revelation 6:9-10, prayers are given for us in heaven from "saints"; 3) elsewhere in Revelation an angel possesses "prayers of the saints" and in turn presents them to God;[3] 4) Jeremiah is described as one who "prays much for the people" after his death in 2 Maccabees 15:13-14.[4] The saints in heaven are clearly aware of earthly happenings. If they have such awareness, it isn't that much of a leap to deduce that they can hear our requests for prayer, especially since the Bible itself shows that they are indeed praying.

We must be careful to avoid silly cultural stereotypes of what heaven is supposedly like. Sometimes we picture clouds, wings, and harps rather than the intensely spiritual place (or state) that it is, with souls longing and burning in their desire for human beings to be saved. The saints who have died devote themselves to prayer for us, because they are perfected in love. They no longer play all the games that we play in order to ignore the spiritual dimension of reality.

A Protestant Might Further Object:

It is not clear how these Catholic practices are any different from the séances, magic, witchcraft, and necromancy forbidden by the Bible. When you come down to it, Catholics are still messing around with dead spirits.

The One-Minute Apologist Says:

Catholics fully agree that these things are prohibited, but deny that the Communion of Saints is a practice included at all in those condemnations.

The difference is in the source of the supernatural power and the intention. When a Christian on earth asks a saint to pray for him (directly supported by the biblical indications above), God is the one whose power makes the relationship between departed and living members of the Body of Christ possible. The medium in a séance, on the other hand, is trying to use her own occult powers to "conjure up" the dead — opening up the very real possibility of demonic counterfeit. Catholics aren't "conjuring" anyone; we're simply asking great departed saints to pray for us. If they are aware of the earth, then God can also make it possible for them to "hear" and heed our prayer requests. If this weren't the case, then saints and angels in heaven wouldn't be portrayed as they are in Scripture: intensely active and still involved in earthly affairs.

✠

"The consoling thing is that while Christendom is divided about the rationality and even the lawfulness, of praying to the saints, we are all agreed about praying with them. . . . You may say that the distinction . . . is not, after all, very great. All the better if so. I sometimes have a bright dream of reunion engulfing us unawares, like a great wave from behind our backs."

C. S. Lewis

[1]Mt. 22:32 [2]Rev. 21:27, 22:14 [3]8:3-4; cf. 5:8, Tob. 12:12, 15 [4]cf. Jer. 15:1

"Venerating" the saints through statues or icons is idolatry

The Bible forbids the use of "graven images," because worship is to be given to God alone.

THE ONE-MINUTE APOLOGIST SAYS:
Statues and icons are fundamentally different from idols, which are expressly intended to replace God.

First of all, veneration of the saints is not worship, which belongs to God only; it is rather an expression of honor — both for the saint and for God, who made the saint holy. This has a solid biblical basis: we are commanded also to honor teachers in the Church,[1] those in the government,[2] and even fellow believers in Christ.[3] Indeed, such a spirit of honoring those who deserve it is supposed to be characteristic of a Christian.[4] The apostle Paul imitated Christ[5] and in turn urged us to imitate him.[6] The Bible also devotes an entire chapter to the heroes of the faith, whom we are to emulate.[7]

Veneration, then, is not at all "unbiblical." But what about the use of statues and icons and other images in the course of such veneration? Exodus 20:4 does prohibit making a "graven image" of God. But what is a "graven image"?

This term is defined in dictionaries as "an idol made of wood or stone." In context, then, it is plain that God was forbidding *idolatry:* making a stone or block of wood into a "god." God told the Jews not to make an image of Him because He revealed Himself as a spirit. Many Bible translations make this crystal-clear by rendering the word as "idol." As if to leave out all doubt, the next verse states: "You shall not bow down to them or serve them" (NIV, NRSV: "worship them").

Worshiping mere blocks of stone or wood is gross idolatry, but this is fundamentally different from using an icon — a visual aid — to worship the one God. Even in the Old Testament the Jews made images of cherubim to decorate the ark of the covenant; they had the bronze serpent in the wilderness, and various images in the decoration of the Temple.

Our Lord and Savior Jesus Christ is described four times in the Bible, by the apostle Paul, as the image (Greek: *eikon*) of God. He applies the word directly to Jesus,[8] and also to describe Christians being transformed into or conformed to the image of Jesus.[9] The Incarnation made images permissible, since Jesus Himself is the "image of the invisible God."[10]

But Catholics go far beyond using images as "visual aids." Isn't it clearly idolatry when a Catholic bows before a statue, or "prays" to a plaster or wooden saint?

THE ONE-MINUTE APOLOGIST SAYS:

If some individual Catholic actually worships Mary as a sort of goddess, or ascribes divine attributes to a saint, he does so contrary to unambiguous Catholic teaching. Some might say that official Catholic teaching aside, it's too easy to see statues or icons as idols or magic charms. But this error is exceedingly rare among Catholics, most of whom understand quite well the function of statues.

This objection is as silly as saying that a person raising his hands up in worship and praise during church is worshiping the ceiling. Why did he use the physical symbolism of "upward" as being directed toward God (since God is everywhere after all)? Why ever kneel when worshiping? Why clasp hands in prayer? These are all physical manifestations of worship toward God. We are physical creatures; when God became man, the physical became involved in the spiritual. Icons and statues help direct our physical, created minds and hearts to the spiritual, uncreated God.

In the Bible we see visual reminders or ritualistic acts used for the purpose of spirituality or devotion to God:

> Numbers 15:38-39: "Speak to the people of Israel, and bid them to make tassels on the corners of their garments throughout their generations, and to put upon the tassel of each corner a cord of blue; and it shall be to you a tassel to look upon and remember all the commandments of the LORD."

Even God speaks (anthropomorphically; that is, as if He were like men, so that we might better understand) of being "reminded" by a visual aid:

> Genesis 9:13-16: "I set my bow in the cloud, and it shall be a sign of the covenant between me and the earth. When I bring clouds over the earth and the bow is seen in the clouds, I will remember my covenant which is between me and you and every living creature of all flesh; and the waters shall never again become a flood to destroy all flesh. When the bow is in the clouds, I will look upon it and remember the everlasting covenant between God and every living creature of all flesh that is upon the earth."

✠

"The attitude of our non-Catholic friends toward the Catholic saints; they always contrive to discredit . . . their witness to the faith: 'Yes, this man was indeed a saint; but then he was not really Roman Catholic. He was just a good Christian. . . . [H]e only happened to be in communion with the Pope because everybody was in those days.'"

RONALD KNOX

[1] 1 Tim. 5:17 [2] Rom. 13:7 [3] 1 Cor. 12:12-26 [4] Rom. 12:10, 1 Pet. 2:17
[5] 1 Cor. 11:1, 1 Thess. 1:6 [6] 1 Cor. 4:16, Phil. 3:17, 2 Thess. 3:7-9 [7] Heb. 11;
cf. 6:12, Jas. 5:10-11 [8] 2 Cor. 4:4, Col. 1:15 [9] Rom. 8:29, 2 Cor. 4:4 [10] Col. 1:15

Other Topics

Indulgences are a way for Catholics to buy salvation and "indulge" themselves in sin

That's why Luther rejected this
corrupt tradition and started the Reformation.

THE ONE-MINUTE APOLOGIST SAYS:
God has granted the Church the power to impose a penalty for
sin (penance), and to forgive sins (absolution) and its penalties (indulgence).

"Indulgence" does not mean a permit to "indulge" in sin. (This would be a very funny notion if it weren't so sadly widespread among non-Catholics.) Rather, indulgences are used by the Catholic Church to extend God's mercy and forgiveness not only to the guilt of sin, but also to its "temporal penalties" — the penance of suffering that must be undergone even after the guilt of sin has been washed away.

It's true that in the Middle Ages there were serious excesses and corruptions surrounding the granting of indulgences, but Catholics believe the core principle is nonetheless valid, because the Bible teaches it, in passages about "binding and loosing." "Binding"[1] meant imposing penalties or not forgiving a sin because of lack of repentance, whereas "loosing" (same passages) meant that a sin was forgiven and (in some cases) its penalties were abolished (an indulgence). The apostle Paul exercises both of these powers in the following passages:

> **1 Corinthians 5:1-5**: "It is actually reported that there is immorality among you, and of a kind that is not found even among pagans; for a man is living with his father's wife. And you are arrogant! Ought you not rather to mourn? Let him who has done this be removed from among you. For though absent in body I am present in spirit, and as if present, I have already pronounced judgment in the name of the Lord Jesus on the man who has done such a thing. When you are assembled, and my spirit is present, with the power of our Lord Jesus, you are to deliver this man to Satan for the destruction of the flesh, that his spirit may be saved in the day of the Lord Jesus."[2]

> **2 Corinthians 2:6-8**: "For such a one this punishment by the majority is enough; so you should rather turn to forgive and comfort him, or he may be overwhelmed by excessive sorrow. So I beg you to reaffirm your love for him."

Paul "binds" in the first passage (penance), and "looses" in the second, where he not only urges the Corinthians to forgive someone on behalf of God (whose judgment was passed through Paul) but also to relax the social stigma that had been put on him for the sake of his repentance and restoration. This act contains all the essential qualities of an indulgence, and involves precisely the same concept.

A PROTESTANT MIGHT FURTHER OBJECT:

But when God forgives our sins, there is no further penalty to pay.[3] Catholics would have God's forgiveness be incomplete, requiring the Church to finish the job.

THE ONE-MINUTE APOLOGIST SAYS:

God's forgiveness is indeed complete. But the Bible teaches that temporal penalties for sin remain even after forgiveness:

> **2 Samuel 12:13-14:** "David said to Nathan, 'I have sinned against the LORD.' And Nathan said to David, 'The LORD also has put away your sin; you shall not die. Nevertheless, because by this deed you have utterly scorned the LORD, the child that is born to you shall die.'"[4]

King David wrote Psalm 103 (about forgiveness), yet when he sinned, he still had to pay a price of suffering, which was directly because of the sin. God cannot change. If He acted in this way in Old Testament times, the principle still applies. Related to this is the purpose of suffering in the Christian life, and particularly God's chastisement. The same Jeremiah who authored Jeremiah 31:34 also wrote the following passage:

> **Jeremiah 31:18-19:** "Thou hast chastened me, and I was chastened, like an untrained calf; bring me back that I may be restored, for thou art the LORD my God. For after I had turned away I repented."[5]

> **Hebrews 12:7:** "It is for discipline that you have to endure. God is treating you as sons; for what son is there whom his father does not discipline?"

This reality remains in New Testament teaching: God, acting through His Church, shows us both discipline and mercy. Indulgences are a wonderful expression of the latter. We should rejoice that God is so merciful.

✝

"We cannot please our opponents. If we fast and give alms; if we crucify our flesh, and make pilgrimages and perform other works of penance, we are accused of clinging to the rags of dead works, instead of 'holding on to Jesus' by faith. If, on the other hand, we enrich our souls with the treasures of Indulgences we are charged with relying on the vicarious merits of others and of lightening too much the salutary burden of the cross. But how can Protestants consistently find fault with the Church for mitigating the austerities of penance, since their own fundamental principle rests on faith alone without good works?"

JAMES CARDINAL GIBBONS

[1]See Mt. 16:19, 18:18, Jn. 20:21-23 [2]cf. 1 Tim. 1:20, Titus 3:10 [3]Ps. 103:12, Jer. 31:34 [4]cf. Num. 14:20-23 [5]cf. Prov. 3:11-12

Formal ritual worship is opposed to a vibrant spiritual life

If we truly love God, we will worship in a spontaneous, heartfelt way, not with rote formulas.

THE ONE-MINUTE APOLOGIST SAYS:
The mere presence of form or ritual has nothing directly to do with whether such worship is heartfelt and "alive" or not. God looks at the heart.

If formal worship or religious ritual were always opposed to a sincere, heartfelt adoration and praise of God, then certainly God wouldn't have commanded it in the Bible. Yet we find that He does exactly that, in many places. Elaborate, painstaking instructions for the Ark of the Covenant,[1] the tabernacle,[2] and the Temple[3] illustrate the highly ritualistic nature of Hebrew worship. A small biblical sampling of some of the religious rituals easily proves that this was extremely formal worship, expressly commanded by God:

> **Leviticus 23:37-38**: "These are the appointed feasts of the LORD, which you shall proclaim as times of holy convocation, for presenting to the LORD offerings by fire, burnt offerings and cereal offerings, sacrifices and drink offerings, each on its proper day; besides the sabbaths of the LORD, and besides your gifts, and besides all your votive offerings, and besides all your freewill offerings, which you give to the LORD."

> **Leviticus 24:5-8**: "And you shall take fine flour, and bake twelve cakes of it; two-tenths of an ephah shall be in each cake. And you shall set them in two rows, six in a row, upon the table of pure gold. And you shall put pure frankincense with each row, that it may go with the bread as a memorial portion to be offered by fire to the LORD. Every sabbath day Aaron shall set it in order before the LORD continually on behalf of the people of Israel as a covenant for ever."

It is true — and was a rather common theme in the Old Testament — that God often warned the people against hypocritical worship: performing of rituals without the proper attitude of heart and spirit toward God. This seems to be an ongoing human tendency; however, we can't possibly conclude from this corruption that all formal rituals ought to be abandoned, since God commanded the worship in the first place. God opposes deceit and hypocrisy, not formality. He instructed the Israelites to perform many sacrifices, so He could hardly despise His own commands. But what He did detest were these rituals performed without the proper attitude and spirit and devotion, or in light of continued sin and disobedience on other grounds:

> **Jeremiah 6:19-20**: "[T]hey have not given heed to my words; and as for my law, they have rejected it. To what purpose does frankincense come to me from Sheba, or sweet cane from a distant land? Your burnt offerings are not acceptable, nor your sacrifices pleasing to me."[4]

> **Amos 5:12, 21-24**: "I know how many are your transgressions, and how great are your sins — you who afflict the righteous, who take a bribe, and turn aside the needy in the gate. . . . I hate, I despise your feasts, and I take no delight in your solemn assemblies. Even though you offer me your burnt offerings and cereal offerings, I will not accept them, and the peace offerings of your fatted beasts I will not look upon. Take away from me the noise of your songs; to the melody of your harps I will not listen. But let justice roll down like waters, and righteousness like an ever-flowing stream."[5]

On the other hand, if the people obeyed His commands, then God was pleased with those same ritual sacrifices.[6]

A PROTESTANT MIGHT FURTHER OBJECT:

But all of that is in the Old Testament. Under the New Covenant, we are to worship from the heart. This eliminates vain rituals, which cannot be found in the New Testament. The Bible thus shows us that worship is now quite informal.

THE ONE-MINUTE APOLOGIST SAYS:

This is untrue. Jesus observed all of the Law. Many scholars believe that the Last Supper was a Passover meal, or at least connected with its preparations.[7] Jesus worshiped in the Temple, in the traditional Jewish manner; for example, during the Feast of Tabernacles.[8] In fact, in the book of Revelation, quite formal and ritualistic ceremonies and worship services are recorded as taking place even in heaven itself,[9] complete with repetitious prayer (Rev. 4:8: "they never cease to sing"), repeated chants or hymns,[10] an altar and incense,[11] and sacrifice.[12]

Thus it is hardly possible to conclude that ritual and formal worship is absent from the New Testament, or that informal worship should be the norm for us today, to the exclusion of formal.

✝

"The prayers of the Church are the age-long poetry of mankind, lifted above the perfection of poetry, for they are the prayer of Christ on earth. That is what the ritual means, with its ordered movements, its wide encircling gestures of love, its kiss of peace, its extended arms of sacrifice."

CARYLL HOUSELANDER (AMERICAN WRITER)

[1]Ex. 25:1-22 [2]Ex. 25:23-40, chs. 26-27 [3]1 Kings 6-7 [4]cf. Mal. 1:6-14
[5]cf. Prov. 15:8, 21:27 [6]e.g., Is. 56:6-7, Jer. 17:24-26, Mal. 1:11 [7]Jn. 13:1
[8]Jn. 7:10-11, 14, 28, 8:2, 20 [9]Rev. 4:8-11, 5:8-14 [10]4:11, 5:9-10 [11]8:3-4 [12]5:6

The Rosary is "vain repetition"

Jesus explicitly condemned and prohibited such
practices, so why do Catholics persist in doing them?

THE ONE-MINUTE APOLOGIST SAYS:
*The Rosary is not a "vain" multiplication of words for
repetition's sake, but a form of prayer, centered on Jesus, that uses
repeated prayers in order to focus concentration and avoid distraction.*

It is often charged that the Rosary is "vain repetition" because certain words are said
over and over ("Hail Mary, full of grace . . ."). It is unnecessary here to delve into all
the details of how the Rosary was designed to work as a meditation on the life of our
Lord. But it is crucial to understand what Jesus meant when He condemned "vain
repetition." Did He have repetition itself in mind?

> **Matthew 6:7**: "And in praying do not heap up empty phrases as the
> Gentiles do; for they think that they will be heard for their many words."
> (KJV: "vain repetitions, as the heathen do . . .")

Clearly repetition per se is not what is prohibited, but "vain repetition" or "empty
phrases." This is different from simply repeating words; it is repeated words for public
consumption, or repeating words for their own sake, without faith. This is seen in
related passages on "vain worship"; for example:

> **Matthew 15:7-9**: "You hypocrites! Well did Isaiah prophesy of you, when he
> said: 'This people honors me with their lips, but their heart is far from me;
> in vain do they worship me, teaching as doctrines the precepts of men.'"[1]

Jesus spoke strongly against worship or devotion that didn't come from the "heart,
soul, strength, and mind":[2] a very common biblical theme, especially in the Old
Testament. Empty, hypocritical religious practice is likewise condemned; for example,
fasting should be done without bringing attention to oneself.[3] Worship without proper
action, and with sin unrepented for, is also to be avoided:

> **James 1:26-27**: "If any one thinks he is religious, and does not bridle his
> tongue but deceives his heart, this man's religion is vain. Religion that is
> pure and undefiled before God and the Father is this: to visit orphans and
> widows in their affliction, and to keep oneself unstained from the world."

Therefore, if one prays the Rosary with the right intention, and a pure heart toward God, there's nothing wrong with it. Indeed, right after His words about "vain repetition," Jesus taught His own form of prayer: the Lord's Prayer, or Our Father,[4] which is repeated by all kinds of Christians (every Sunday, by many). Jesus Himself utilized repetition, too: for example, He repeated the same prayer three times in the Garden of Geth-semane.[5] It was a common Hebrew way of emphasizing a certain theme; a memory aid. In the Sermon on the Mount, for example, He repeats the phrase "Blessed are . . . for they shall / for theirs is . . ." nine times.[6]

A Protestant Might Further Object:

Granted, there is some repetition in the Bible, but are there entire sentences repeated over and over (almost chant-like) as in the Rosary? If not, isn't it reasonable to suppose that something like the Rosary was being condemned?

The One-Minute Apologist Says:

That could hardly be the case, since in Psalm 136, the same exact phrase, "for His steadfast love endures for ever" is repeated through the entire Psalm, for twenty-six straight verses. That's two-and-a-half times more repetition than the ten Hail Marys recited in the Rosary at any one time. Other phrases also recur throughout this meditation and praise to God: "O give thanks" in verses 1-3, then reiterated in verse 26; "to Him who" eight times, in verses 4-7, 10, 13, 16-17. This format is often used in Hebrew poetic literature (which was also used for worship, as in the case of the Psalms):

> **Psalm 136:1-7:** "O give thanks to the LORD, for He is good, for His stead-fast love endures for ever. O give thanks to the God of gods, for His stead-fast love endures for ever. O give thanks to the Lord of lords, for His steadfast love endures for ever; to Him who alone does great wonders, for His steadfast love endures for ever; to Him who by understanding made the heavens, for His steadfast love endures for ever; to Him who spread out the earth upon the waters, for His steadfast love endures for ever; to Him who made the great lights, for His steadfast love endures for ever."

Worship in heaven is also presented as intensely repetitious: "Day and night they never cease to sing, 'Holy, holy, holy, is the Lord God Almighty, who was and is and is to come!'"[7] Since such repetition is a common biblical theme, the repetition of prayers in the Rosary cannot be condemned on biblical grounds. "Vain repetition" clearly refers to a particular kind of repetition, with the emphasis on the "vain."

✝

"Repeated prayers are not necessarily mechanical. A pianist like Paderewski may play the same concerto over and over again and always play it with a perfect interpretation; an actor like Forbes Robertson may play the part of Hamlet night after night for months, and always reveal some new meaning in his lines."

Bertrand L. Conway

[1]cf. Mk. 7:6-7 [2]Lk. 10:27 [3]Mt. 7:16-18 [4]Mt. 6:8-13
[5]Mt. 26:39, 42, 44 [6]Mt. 5:3-11 [7]Rev. 4:8; cf. Is. 6:3

Crucifixes prove that Catholics believe Jesus is not yet glorified in heaven

Jesus is risen! So why do Catholics
focus so much on His crucified body?

THE ONE-MINUTE APOLOGIST SAYS:

*Jesus is indeed risen. But crucifixes help us to remember the central
and most important event in history: Jesus' redemptive death on the Cross.*

A Catholic pondering Jesus by means of gazing upon a crucifix (a cross with a three-dimensional image of our Lord dying on it) no more proves that Catholics deny or downplay Jesus' Resurrection, Ascension, and glorification, than a manger scene in a Protestant church at Christmas "proves" that a Protestant thinks Jesus is still a baby. In both cases, visual aids are used to foster devotion and meditation on some aspect of the life of Jesus.

In both cases the symbol calls to mind a Christian mystery. The manger represents the Incarnation: Jesus coming to earth, taking on flesh, and becoming a man.[1] The crucifix obviously brings to mind what Jesus did for sinful men, on the Cross — without which there would have been no resurrection.

If Christians were only permitted to worship the "risen Jesus" or the glorified Jesus in heaven, then why would He Himself accept such worship on earth?[2] He was also worshiped as a baby.[3] Jesus remains God at all times: before the Incarnation, during it, and after He ascended to heaven. Furthermore, the Bible plainly teaches us that Jesus was worshiped as a slain Lamb in heaven, after He was glorified.[4] So His glorification in heaven clearly does not prohibit worship of Him while pondering His sacrificial death on the Cross.

A PROTESTANT MIGHT FURTHER OBJECT:

But if it were so important to dwell upon the Crucifixion, wouldn't the Bible stress this? Instead, we are told to devote our minds to the Risen Jesus: we are after all a "Resurrection People."

THE ONE-MINUTE APOLOGIST SAYS:

The apostle Paul, St. Peter, and the author of Hebrews did indeed emphasize such worship, and nowhere indicate that only the risen, glorified Jesus should be worshiped and meditated upon. In fact, quite the contrary:

Romans 6:3-8: "Do you not know that all of us who have been baptized into Christ Jesus were baptized into His death? We were buried therefore with Him by baptism into death, so that as Christ was raised from the dead by the glory of the Father, we too might walk in newness of life. For if we have been united with Him in a death like His, we shall certainly be united with Him in a resurrection like His. We know that our old self was crucified with Him so that the sinful body might be destroyed, and we might no longer be enslaved to sin. For he who has died is freed from sin. But if we have died with Christ, we believe that we shall also live with Him."[5]

1 Corinthians 1:17-18, 23: "For Christ did not send me to baptize but to preach the gospel, and not with eloquent wisdom, lest the Cross of Christ be emptied of its power. For the word of the cross is folly to those who are perishing, but to us who are being saved it is the power of God. . . . [B]ut we preach Christ crucified, a stumbling block to Jews and folly to Gentiles."[6]

1 Corinthians 2:1-2: "When I came to you, brethren, I did not come proclaiming to you the testimony of God in lofty words or wisdom. For I decided to know nothing among you except Jesus Christ and Him crucified."

Galatians 6:14: "But far be it from me to glory except in the Cross of our Lord Jesus Christ, by which the world has been crucified to me, and I to the world."

Hebrews 12:2-3: "[L]ooking to Jesus the pioneer and perfecter of our faith, who for the joy that was set before Him endured the Cross, despising the shame, and is seated at the right hand of the throne of God. Consider Him who endured from sinners such hostility against Himself, so that you may not grow weary or fainthearted."[7]

Despite what Protestant traditions sometimes contend, when Catholics make use of crucifixes to pursue meditation on the saving mystery of the Cross, and Jesus' death, they do so according to a sound biblical model.

✠

"Now we do not request more than that one permit us to regard a crucifix or a saint's image as a witness, for remembrance, as a sign as that image of Caesar was. Should it not be as possible for us without sin to have a crucifix or an image of Mary, as it was for the Jews and Christ himself to have an image of Caesar who, pagan and now dead, belonged to the Devil?"

MARTIN LUTHER

[1]Jn. 1:14, 1 Tim. 3:16 [2]Mt. 8:2, 9:18, 14:33, Jn. 5:23, 20:28, etc.
[3]Mt. 2:2, 11, Heb. 1:6 [4]Rev. 5:6-14 [5]cf. 2 Cor. 1:5-7, 4:10,
Gal. 2:20, Phil. 3:10 [6]cf. Gal. 5:11 [7]cf. 1 Pet. 2:19-21

Catholic "sacramentals" and relics are unbiblical magic

The Bible teaches that grace and salvation come through the spirit, not through "holy objects."

THE ONE-MINUTE APOLOGIST SAYS:
The Incarnation of Jesus elevated the dignity of matter, making it a means of conveying grace.

His death on the Cross was also intensely physical. Protestants often speak of "the blood" (Ephesians 1:7: "In Him we have redemption through His blood"; Hebrews 9:12: "His own blood, thus securing an eternal redemption"; 1 Peter 1:2: "sprinkling with His blood"; 1 John 1:7: "the blood of Jesus His Son cleanses us from all sin," etc.); this is but one of many examples of "sacramentalism."

The New Testament is filled with many concrete examples or teachings about the "incarnational principle" and sacramentalism. Baptism confers regeneration.[1] Jesus' garment,[2] saliva mixed with dirt,[3] and water from the pool of Siloam[4] all were used in healings. Anointing with oil for healing is also prescribed.[5] The Bible often calls for a laying on of hands for the purpose of ordination and commissioning[6] and in order to heal.[7]

Even relics (remnants of the bodies of saints and holy people, and related physical items), have (perhaps surprisingly) strong biblical support. Perhaps the most striking proof text is a story about the prophet Elisha:

> **2 Kings 13:20-21**: "So Eli'sha died, and they buried him. Now bands of Moabites used to invade the land in the spring of the year. And as a man was being buried, lo, a marauding band was seen and the man was cast into the grave of Eli'sha; and as soon as the man touched the bones of Eli'sha, he revived, and stood on his feet."

Examples of second-class relics (objects that came into contact with holy people) are also clearly found in passages about the prophet Elijah's mantle, which parted the Jordan River,[8] and Peter's shadow,[9] and even Paul's handkerchief,[10] which God used to heal sick people and to cast out demons. If all of this is "magic," then it would have to be a sort of "magic" directly sanctioned by God Himself. But it's not magic: it is biblical sacramentalism — God's use of matter to convey grace.

A Protestant Might Further Object:

What cannot be found in the Bible, however, is the veneration of relics. This goes too far, and it is idolatry. The Bible does tell us that we can remember the deeds of great heroes of the faith (following Acts 7 and Hebrews 11) and thank God for them, but we shouldn't get into worshiping bones or pieces of hair and so forth, or go on pilgrimages to "holy places." That's too much like paganism or heathenism and adds nothing to our spiritual life. All places are equally "holy."

The One-Minute Apologist Says:

If matter can indeed impart grace and blessing, according to the Bible, then we can give glory to God for what He has done with lowly matter by venerating (not worshiping) even now-inanimate objects. Protestants themselves would not, for example, think that the birthplace of Jesus in Bethlehem, or the hill where He died on the Cross, or His tomb, from which He rose from the dead, are merely rocks and dirt like any other rocks and dirt (if all places are "equally holy," would a Protestant bulldoze Calvary and make it a parking lot or a gas station?). In their own way Protestants do indeed venerate and honor them, and the land of Israel in their heads, in "spirit."

Plenty of Protestants are also fascinated and intrigued by the Shroud of Turin, which is an extraordinary secondary relic related to our Lord Jesus. That is an object, too; a mere piece of cloth. But would any Christian treat it like any other cloth and tear it up for rags to dust with? Of course they would not, because it was connected with Jesus and has miraculous properties (like Elisha's bones): a supernaturally produced image. Therefore it is highly regarded and revered. It all goes back to God and His great works, using matter. Sacramentalism and relics flow from the Incarnation: God Himself taking on flesh and matter and becoming man.

Imagine, for example, if by some extraordinary process, we were sure that we had in our possession, some of St. Paul's handkerchiefs. Would they be treated like any run-of-the-mill napkin or kitchen apron? Of course not. Even non-believers would at least respect them as historical items and display them in a museum. And most Protestants would cherish them, as a possession of the great evangelist. But it seems that the Bible would urge us to go one step further than that. Why would it be improper to believe that these items may still have the power to heal that they had in apostolic times? I see nothing in the Bible that would forbid such a possible use, in faith. And if we venerated these material items, it would be precisely because we are glorifying God, who used them to perform miracles.

✛

"[D]ivine power works invisibly through visible signs. . . . Hereby is excluded the error of certain heretics, who wish all visible sacramental signs swept away. . . . These visible sacramental signs are the instruments of a God Incarnate and Crucified."

St. Thomas Aquinas (1225-1274)

[1]Acts 2:38, 22:16, 1 Pet. 3:21; cf. Mk. 16:16, Rom. 6:3-4, 1 Cor. 6:11, Titus 3:5
[2]Mt. 9:20-22 [3]Jn. 9:5 ff., Mk. 8:22-25 [4]Jn. 9:7 [5]Jas. 5:14 [6]Acts 6:6 [7]Mk. 6:5,
Lk. 13:13 [8]2 Kings 2:11-14 [9]Acts 5:15-16 [10]Acts 19:11-12

Marriage is not absolutely indissoluble

Jesus Himself permitted divorce under certain conditions
— for example, adultery — so why don't Catholics?

THE ONE-MINUTE APOLOGIST SAYS:
*Jesus actually took a very strict line on marriage and the
impermissibility of divorce. The supposed "exception for adultery"
based on Matthew 19:9 is a misinterpretation of the biblical text.*

Traditionally, Protestants have also held to a very strict prohibition of divorce, but over
the years — especially in the last century — many denominations have allowed for
more and more situations where it is permitted. But the Catholic Church has consistently taught that a valid, sacramental marriage is indissoluble for as long as both
spouses are alive. Jesus' own words on this subject are very clear:

Matthew 19:3-6: "And Pharisees came up to Him and tested Him by asking, 'Is it lawful to divorce one's wife for any cause?' He answered, 'Have
you not read that He who made them from the beginning made them
male and female, and said, "For this reason a man shall leave his father
and mother and be joined to his wife, and the two shall become one
flesh"? So they are no longer two but one flesh. What therefore God has
joined together, let not man put asunder.'"[1]

Mark 10:11-12: "Whoever divorces his wife and marries another, commits
adultery against her; and if she divorces her husband and marries another,
she commits adultery."[2]

1 Corinthians 7:10-11, 39: "To the married I give charge, not I but the
Lord, that the wife should not separate from her husband (but if she does,
let her remain single or else be reconciled to her husband) — and that the
husband should not divorce his wife. . . . A wife is bound to her husband
as long as he lives."[3]

The key to understanding the biblical teaching is to realize that "becoming one
flesh" (as occurs in a consummated, valid, sacramental marriage) is an irreversible state
of affairs. It is no more reversible than it is possible to unscramble an egg (to use a
rather crude analogy), because "God has joined [them] together."

A Protestant Might Further Object:

But Jesus made an exception for "unchastity" — meaning adultery. How do Catholics reconcile Jesus' words with their church's teaching?

The One-Minute Apologist Says:

Some indeed think that Jesus allowed an exception for adultery when he said, "Whoever divorces his wife, except for unchastity, and marries another, commits adultery."[4] At first glance, this does appear to be a "loophole."

This problem of the seeming differences between Matthew and the other Gospels and St. Paul's epistles has vexed Bible scholars for centuries, giving rise to numerous attempts at explanation or reconciliation. Some think that the alleged "exceptions" in Matthew were directed specifically at Jewish believers still bound to Mosaic Law. Another significant strain of scholarly opinion holds that the controversial passages in Matthew were later interpolations (thus not truly authentic biblical texts), attempting to soften the absolute prohibition of divorce that was deemed too difficult to follow.

But Catholics believe that such verses refer to a "marriage" which was in fact never a true marriage at all — and thus not an indissoluble union. This interpretation is the only one that squares logically with the strong statements against divorce that Jesus makes elsewhere. The entire body of Jesus' teaching about marriage and divorce points to the conclusion that marriage is indissoluble and divorce impossible; therefore this "exception clause" must refer to something other than marriage.

A solid basis for this understanding can be established by examining the Greek words used. The word for "unchastity" in Matthew 5:32 and 19:9 is *porneia*, which is rarely ever translated as "adultery" (the Greek word for this is *moicheia*) but rather usually as "fornication." Jesus was not referring to married spouses who are unfaithful, but to men and women who weren't actually married in the first place; they were committing fornication, not adultery. Thus there was no obstacle to their separating.

But even in cases of separation or even civil divorce, the Church Fathers, and also many Protestants (until very recent times), did not allow a second marriage. The only allowable condition for a second marriage was when the spouse died. If divorce is indeed impermissible, no second marriage can take place; in fact, it would be a misnomer to call it a "marriage" at all; it would be a state of ongoing adultery.

Even so, there is no obstacle to a Catholic obtaining a civil divorce; if, for example, there is a terrible problem such as spousal abuse or a situation requiring physical separation for the health and well-being of one of the partners. But there can be no further marriage unless an annulment is obtained, signifying that no valid, sacramental marriage was truly present from the beginning.

✟

"The sacramental bond, which they lose neither through separation nor through adultery, this the spouses should guard chastely and harmoniously."

St. Augustine

[1]cf. Mk. 10:6-9 [2]cf. Mt. 5:32b, Lk. 16:18 [3]cf. 6:9 [4]Mt. 19:9; cf. 5:32a

"Annulments" are just the Catholic rationalization for divorce

Regardless of what their Church teaches about marriage, Catholics get divorced like everyone else; they just give it a different name.

THE ONE-MINUTE APOLOGIST SAYS:
Annulment is, in fact, a fundamentally different concept from divorce, and has support in the Bible and parallels even in civil law.

A divorce presumes that a marriage existed and could be ended. An annulment, in contrast, is a declaration by the Church that a true, sacramental marriage never took place at all, because certain necessary conditions were not present. Even secular law recognizes this distinction, as any encyclopedia entry for "annulment" will show you. We see this difference in Scripture, too; for example, the distinction between a concubine and a wife.[1] Many Israelites "put away" their ostensible wives on the grounds that the "marriages" were illegitimate, based on Mosaic Law:

> **Ezra 9:14**: "Shall we break thy commandments again and intermarry with the peoples who practice these abominations?"

> **Ezra 10:2-3, 10-11, 19**: "'We have broken faith with our God and have married foreign women from the peoples of the land, but even now there is hope for Israel in spite of this. Therefore let us make a covenant with our God to put away all these wives and their children, according to the counsel of my lord and of those who tremble at the commandment of our God; and let it be done according to the law.' . . . And Ezra the priest stood up and said to them, 'You have trespassed and married foreign women, and so increased the guilt of Israel. Now then make confession to the LORD, the God of your fathers, and do His will; separate yourselves from the peoples of the land and from the foreign wives.' . . . They pledged themselves to put away their wives."

This occurred not simply because the wives were ethnically different, but because they brought with them the influence of idolatry and false religion.[2] Foreigners who kept Jewish Law were to be welcomed,[3] and Jews were not prohibited from marrying foreign women per se.[4] But the particular "marriages" decried in Ezra were not allowed by God, hence, they weren't true marriages from the start: exactly the same thing as a Catholic annulment. Accordingly, Abraham sent away Hagar and her son Ishmael,[5] not because they were evil or disparaged by God,[6] but because Sarah was Abraham's wife in the fuller sense (akin to sacramental marriage).

The distinction between a concubine and a wife bears further examination because it offers somewhat of an analogy (although not a perfect one) to annulment. Mosaic Law offered concubines legal protection: similar to civil legal protection today of a woman later determined by the Church to be in a non-sacramental "marriage."[7] Yet they were regarded differently from wives,[8] and it was easier to obtain (in effect) a "divorce" from them (e.g., Abraham's concubine Hagar in Genesis 21:10-14). It's interesting that the Old Testament frequently contrasts "wives" with "concubines" in the same sentence.[9] One finds remarkable instances of the Jewish kings' taking dozens of wives and even hundreds of concubines. Setting aside the separate complex issue of Old Testament polygamy, it is worthwhile to note that in Scripture there is such a thing as a sexual relationship that is not technically a marriage. This is similar in many ways to an ostensible "marriage" which is later annulled as no true marriage.

A PROTESTANT MIGHT FURTHER OBJECT:

But wasn't that a unique situation in Old Testament times? God was taking extra measures to protect His people from foreign non-Jewish religious corruption. But after the time of Jesus, God no longer restricted marriage in that fashion after the time of Jesus. It still seems that annulments are just a Catholic version of divorce.

THE ONE-MINUTE APOLOGIST SAYS:

God doesn't change. If God reveals that something is wrong, it cannot later become right. If God Himself gives requirements for a valid marriage, these will transcend times and cultures. These may change, but the fundamental, inherent nature of marriage does not, because it is rooted in God's word and in fundamental human nature.

In light of the requirements for valid marriage, the concept of annulments is eminently commonsensical. Surely not every single marriage ceremony results in a validly married couple. One or both parties might be under coercion, already married, or of unsound mind. They might be grossly ignorant of (or interiorly opposed to) what they are consenting to, or be too closely related by blood. The form of the ceremony might be seriously defective, and so on. The Catholic annulment process includes an investigation to determine if factors such as these were present.

✛

"Is there no difference between tearing up a genuine fifty-dollar bill (the state divorce) and declaring another fifty-dollar bill a counterfeit (the Church annulment)?"

BERTRAND L. CONWAY

---

[1]Gen. 21:10-14, Judges 8:30-31 [2]Dt. 17:17, Ezra 9:1-2, Neh. 13:23-28 [3]Lev. 19:33-34, Num. 15:13-16 [4]Dt. 21:10-13 [5]Gen. 21:12 [6]Gen. 17:20, 21:13, 17-20 [7]Ex. 21:7-11, Dt. 21:10-14 [8]Jude 8:30-31 [9]e.g., 2 Sam. 5:13, 19:5

The Catholic ban on contraception is an arbitrary, unbiblical restriction

It's just one of many areas where the Catholic Church imposes burdensome traditions of men upon its flock.

THE ONE-MINUTE APOLOGIST SAYS:

Contraception was commonly prohibited by all Christians — Protestant, Orthodox, and Catholic — until 1930. It is a biblical and patristic belief.

Here is the classic biblical passage having to do with contraception:

Genesis 38:8-10: "Then Judah said to Onan, 'Go in to your brother's wife, and perform the duty of a brother-in-law to her, and raise up off-spring for your brother.' But Onan knew that the offspring would not be his; so when he went in to his brother's wife he spilled the semen on the ground, lest he should give offspring to his brother. And what he did was displeasing in the sight of the LORD, and He slew him also."

This story involved what is known as the "levirate law": the duty to produce off-spring with the wife of a dead brother. Onan failed to uphold this law, but that alone cannot be why God killed him, since we know from Deuteronomy 25:5-10 that the penalty for that was public humiliation and shunning, not death. (Indeed, later in the same chapter Onan's father refuses to enforce the law and allow his other son, Shelah, to produce a child with Tamar, his daughter-in-law. Judah acknowledges his sin, yet neither he nor Shelah is killed for it.) No, Onan was judged for contraception (sex with the deliberate intent to unnaturally prevent procreation), and in a sign of the gravity of that crime, God struck him down for it.

Providing implicit support for Catholic teaching are a host of other biblical passages that exalt fertility and the blessing of many children, and the curse of none:

1) Married couples are to "be fruitful and multiply"; this is a blessing.[1]

2) Barrenness is contrary to blessing and "glory."[2]

3) Procreation is central to marriage.[3]

4) Childbearing is so sacred that women are even said to be "saved" by it.[4]

5) It is God who opens and closes wombs and causes a conception to occur.[5]

6) Children are a gift from God.[6]

A Protestant Might Further Object:

But this is an outdated understanding of the meaning of marriage and parenthood.

Today we know that marriage is primarily about love — not about having babies. Moreover, having ten or more children might have worked in ancient agrarian societies, but it's unreasonable in a modern, urban world that is already suffering from overpopulation.

The One-Minute Apologist Says:

The Catholic Church doesn't force married couples to have ten, or any specific number of children! But it does require them to agree to be fruitful and always open to life, in order to fulfill the deepest meaning and purpose of marital union. For having children is not meant to be separated from marital love, but to be a full and everlasting expression of it.

The problem today isn't too many families having "ten or more children," but rather, too many having too few — or none at all. In most Christian countries (including essentially all of Europe), birth rates are so low that there is actually negative population growth. This poses a major threat to the economic and cultural future of these nations. According to the ultimately selfish, "anti-child" mentality that fuels contraception, children are often viewed as a mere inconvenience or a burden — even to the point of being slaughtered before they are born. (Any pro-life Christian must lament how abortion is often sadly employed as a "backup" to contraception.)

The Bible, on the other hand, clearly states over and over that children (and many of them) are a blessing. Yet, sadly, millions of Christians today are far closer in outlook to secular (or ancient pagan) culture than the biblical worldview:

> **1 Chronicles 25:5:** "All these were the sons of Heman the king's seer, according to the promise of God to exalt him; for God had given Heman fourteen sons and three daughters."

> **Psalm 127:3-5:** "Lo, sons are a heritage from the LORD, the fruit of the womb a reward. Like arrows in the hand of a warrior are the sons of one's youth. Happy is the man who has his quiver full of them!"

✠

"It has been left to the last Christians, or rather to the first Christians fully committed to blaspheming and denying Christianity, to invent a new kind of worship of Sex, which is not even a worship of Life. It has been left to the very latest Modernists to proclaim an erotic religion which at once exalts lust and forbids fertility. . . . The new priests abolish the fatherhood and keep the feast — to themselves."

G. K. Chesterton

[1]Gen. 1:28, 9:1, 7, 28:3, 35:11, Dt. 7:13-14, Ps. 107:38, 115:14, 128:1-4,
Prov. 17:6, Ecc. 6:3 [2]Ex. 23:25-26, Jer. 18:21, Hos. 9:11 [3]Mal. 2:14-15
[4]1 Tim. 2:15 [5]Gen. 20:17-18, 29:31, 30:2, 22, Josh. 24:3-4, Ruth 4:13,
Ps. 113:9 [6]Gen. 17:16, 20, 29:32-33, 33:5, Ps. 127:3

Dave Armstrong

Dave Armstrong is a Catholic writer, apologist, and evangelist who has been actively proclaiming and defending Christianity for more than twenty years. Formerly a campus missionary, as a Protestant, Armstrong was received into the Catholic Church in 1991 by the late, well-known catechist and theologian Fr. John A. Hardon, S.J.

Armstrong's conversion story appeared in the best-selling book *Surprised by Truth,* and his articles have been published in a number of Catholic periodicals, including *The Catholic Answer, This Rock, Envoy, Hands On Apologetics, The Coming Home Journal,* and *The Latin Mass.* His apologetic and writing apostolate was the subject of a feature article in the May 2002 issue of *Envoy.* Armstrong is the author of the books *A Biblical Defense of Catholicism* and *More Biblical Evidence for Catholicism* and of forty-four apologetics articles in *The Catholic Answer Bible.*

His website, Biblical Evidence for Catholicism (www.biblicalcatholic.com), online since March 1997, received the 1998 Catholic Website of the Year award from *Envoy,* which also nominated Armstrong himself for Best New Evangelist.

Armstrong, his wife, Judy, and their four children live near Detroit, Michigan.

An Invitation

Reader, the book that you hold in your hands was published by Sophia Institute Press.

Sophia Institute seeks to restore man's knowledge of eternal truth, including man's knowledge of his own nature, his relation to other persons, and his relation to God.

Our press fulfills this mission by offering translations, reprints, and new publications. We offer scholarly as well as popular publications; there are works of fiction along with books that draw from all the arts and sciences of our civilization. These books afford readers a rich source of the enduring wisdom of mankind.

Sophia Institute Press is the publishing arm of the Thomas More College of Liberal Arts and Holy Spirit College. Both colleges are dedicated to providing university-level education in the Western tradition under the guiding light of Catholic teaching.

If you know a young person who might be interested in the ideas found in this book, share it. If you know a young person seeking a college that takes seriously the adventure of learning and the quest for truth, bring our institutions to his attention.

www.SophiaInstitute.com
www.ThomasMoreCollege.edu
www.HolySpiritCollege.org

SOPHIA INSTITUTE PRESS

THE PUBLISHING DIVISION OF